John D. Larkin: A Business Pioneer

by Daniel Irving Larkin

To Carrie Best wishes Wm Larkin

Daniel I. Larkin
389 Getzville Road
Amherst, New York 14226

Cover design by Eberle-Sciandra, Buffalo, N.Y.. Commemorative medal
issued May 1, 1925 for the 50th anniversary of the founding of the
Larkin Company.

Second printing, February, 1999

Printed in the United States on acid free paper
by BookCrafters, Chelsea, MI. 48118

Library of Congress Preassigned Catalog Card No. 98-091231

ISBN 0-9619697-1-7

Also by Daniel I. Larkin

Dear Will: Letters from the China Trade 1833–1836

Acknowledgments

This book has been in the making over a period of years and many people have contributed to it. My late brother, Harry H. Larkin Jr., who presided over the final dissolution of John D. Larkin's business, saved from the files in the President's Office a large number of documents, photographs and scrap albums which cover the history of the Larkin Company from its founding in 1875 down to the end in 1967. This collection is now in the Library of the Buffalo and Erie County Historical Society. My cousin, Elizabeth Robb Duane, turned over to me a valuable collection of letters, diaries and scrapbooks relative to the lives of John D. Larkin and Frances Hubbard Larkin. Without these two resources this story could never have been told.

To Professor Jack Quinan of the SUNY at Buffalo Department of Architecture I cannot adequately express my thanks for his constant encouragement, his insightful participation in lengthy discussions of the subject matter, and his careful reading of the manuscript.

I am deeply indebted to Mary Bell, Librarian, and the staff of the Buffalo and Erie County Historical Society Library for their patience and unfailing help with this project. I am equally indebted to Shonnie Finnegan and Christopher Densmore of the SUNY at Buffalo Archives for their help with the Darwin D. Martin papers. My thanks to William H. Loos, curator of the Rare Book Room, Buffalo and Erie County Public Library, for the help he has given in locating primary sources in the collection.

I owe a special thanks to Diane Benison who typeset the book and wrote the index. Her patience and expertise made this publication possible. Thanks, too, to my daughters, Penelope, Sarah, and Elizabeth who brought me into the age of the computer and contributed much to the making of this book.

Finally, more thanks than I can say to my wife, Peggy, who read, and re-read and encouraged over a long and tedious gestation until the John D. Larkin story finally saw the light.

John D. Larkin: A Business Pioneer

John D. Larkin, 1913.
This photo was first published in *The Larkin Idea*, March, 1913.

Contents

Prologue

Today as we look back at the first quarter of the twentieth century the twenties seem to mark the true beginning of the modern era. World War I lay behind us, and the future seemed to hold unlimited promise. With Calvin Coolidge firmly established in the White House, the American economy was booming, and significant social and technological changes seemed to promise a glowing future. Women had gained the vote and been emancipated from the cumbersome fashions of the Victorian and Edwardian eras. The flapper had taken center stage with her bobbed hair, short skirts, rolled stockings, cloche hats, and cigarette holder. Valentino was all the rage. It was the era chronicled by F. Scott Fitzgerald in *The Great Gatsby*, the era of jazz and bootleg liquor and a daring new dance, the Charleston. More significantly, perhaps, the harnessing of electricity, at the end of the nineteenth century had brought in the telephone, the telegraph and finally radio. The Model T made the automobile available to the average family. Airplanes were carrying mail across the country and transatlantic flight lay just around the corner. Distances were suddenly less significant, and all the marvels of science that had been accumulating since the previous century seemed to promise a bountiful future for America. Progress was here and now and seemed forever.

On Friday, May 1, 1925, there was an unusual stir of activity throughout the great factory buildings and the now legendary Frank Lloyd Wright administration building of Larkin Co Inc. at 680 Seneca Street in Buffalo, New York. The day marked the fiftieth anniversary of the founding of the Company in 1875, and members of the Larkin business family were preparing a gala celebration. There was much to celebrate.

In those fifty years, Larkin Company had grown from a small local soap manufactory into one of the largest mail order houses in the country. Thousands of housewives across the country had come to depend on Larkin merchandise to stock their cupboards, furnish their homes and clothe their families. The Larkin catalog offered in its several hundred pages two kinds of merchandise—products and premiums. The products consisted of a wide variety of soaps and cleansers, perfumes and cosmetics, pharmaceutical items and food products. The majority of the 900 products offered were manufactured in the factories on Seneca Street. The premiums included furniture, clothing, household utensils, rugs, lamps, radios, phonographs, paints—in short most of what one might expect to find in a large mail order catalog today. As with the products, many of the premiums were manufactured in the Larkin factory, and a large number were made for the company locally or out of town, either by wholly owned subsidiaries or manufacturers who were able to supply the large quantities required by the company. In addition to its Buffalo offices, Larkin Company had branches in Peoria, Chicago, Cleveland, Pittsburgh, New York, and Boston. The slogan that built the business was "Factory to Family," a concept that is having a resurgence in the Factory Outlet Malls so popular today. The basic concept behind such merchandising was incorporated in the Larkin slogan: "Eliminate all cost that adds no value." By 1925, Larkin Company had expanded in several directions beyond its mail order business. A complete department store had been opened on Seneca Street. Larkin Hammerless Gas was sold in Larkin gas stations in Buffalo, Rochester, and Erie, Pennsylvania. One hundred and fifty four Larkin Chain Stores brought Larkin products and fresh produce to the residents of Buffalo, western New York, and Peoria, Illinois. Larkin Co Inc. employed over 2,000 Buffalonians, and the branches and subsidiary companies added another 2,000 to the total payroll.

That Friday in May, 1925, the Larkinites, as the employees proudly called themselves, did indeed have something to celebrate in what they called their "Fifty Golden Years." The great office building was buzzing with more than usual activity. Although business would be transacted during the ceremonies, each department head had arranged to release some members to tend to arrangements. Girls from various departments came in early to put the finishing touches on the preparations. They placed in Mr. Larkin's office and elsewhere the many flower arrangements that filled the offices with their color and fragrance. Against a background of purple velvet, they set up the wreath with a large gold "50" in its center on the partition behind the president's desk. On the table behind his desk chair, they placed the 20-inch gold-lined silver cup that was the gift of the employees to their beloved founder. Chairs and music stands were arranged around the piano in the light court near the elevators (probably where the organ console would eventually go) for the members of the Y.W.C.A. Orchestra and the Larkin String Orchestra. Each group had been rehearsing programs to present during the morning. Managers in each department of the office and the factory had arranged the work so that every employee would have an opportunity to go to the president's office during the day to greet Mr. Larkin personally. The heads of the branches in Chicago, Peoria and Philadelphia had all come to Buffalo to participate. One of the highlights of the festivities would be the presentation to Mr. Larkin of a folio-size book containing the signatures of all the Larkin employees throughout the country.

Who was this man who would be the recipient of so much love and attention this first day of May, 1925? John Durrant Larkin was a man of medium height and build with snow white hair and a full beard neatly trimmed in the fashion of the Edwardian era. He would be 80 years old the following September, but his brisk step and bright eyes belied his age. He rarely missed a day at the office—"the works" as he was wont to call the plant—and then only when he travelled abroad or tended to the business of his farms in Canada. A glance through *Ourselves*, the employee publication, or a conversation with anyone who had worked at Larkin Company, reveals at once that he was loved by all for his friendliness and kindness, and admired for his modesty, integrity and generosity.[1] He was a hard worker himself, but never a slave driver, and the welfare of his employees always came first. Cooperation, rather than competition, was the watchword in his business. John D. Larkin came of English stock, and he conducted himself towards others with the dignity and courtesy that one associates with the true English gentleman. He was reserved, but always kind and caring. With all this, he was a man who knew the value of play. He promoted opportunities for recreation among his employees—athletic teams, picnics, musical events—and in the early days provided a piano in the office to break the monotony of desk work. There are pictures of John playing tennis with his family or riding a bicycle, and he greatly enjoyed playing cards with his grandchildren after a day at the office. John was never a man to waste his energy on worry or to react to a situation with fear. Once, in his later years, a watchman and a burglar exchanged gunfire in the front hall of his home. John, busy in his office off the hall, heard the commotion and stepped out into the line of fire. The burglar escaped. When asked if he was hurt, John "coolly replied: 'No, I guess not. I believe I am allright.' He displayed not the slightest semblance of excitement."[2] This, then, was the man whose arrival the two thousand employees at the Larkin plant eagerly awaited that morning in May.

Punctually at a little before 10:00 o'clock Charles Pratt, long-time employee and coachman turned chauffeur, pulled the Larkin car up to the curb at 680 Seneca Street. John stepped briskly out and walked purposefully up the long red sandstone steps and through the large plate glass doors that opened into the lobby. He knew that some celebration was afoot, and that he would be expected to use the formal entrance rather than the tower door that led more directly to his office. Once inside, he was greeted by two old friends, Darwin D. Martin and Miss Kaiser. Martin had come to work for John as a boy in 1878 , and Miss Kaiser of Central Sales was the senior woman employee.[3] These two escorted the president to his office where he was greeted by his sons John Jr. and Harry, and his son-in-law Walter B. Robb. The small office space was filled with banks of flowers, and behind his desk stood the large silver loving cup engraved in his honor. *Ourselves* reports: "It was a complete surprise to him, and if Larkinites could have seen how genuinely pleased and touched he was, they could have wished that it might have been ten times costlier and larger."[4]

The girls of the Y.W.C.A Orchestra had already taken their places under the direction of Joseph A. Ball, and their music filled the great court beyond John's office. At the same time the column of employees from the factory and the office began to form, and for the remainder of the morning a steady stream of well-wishers filed past the president's desk. John greeted each one with a smile, a word of recognition, and a bronze commemorative medal with his portrait and signature on one side and the image of the factory, the company logo, and the dates 1875 and 1925 on the other. Many were old friends who, like Darwin Martin, had shared the fortunes of the company with him from the early days, some he would meet for the first time, but all had the same warm reception. For over three hours John stood by his desk and greeted the members of his business family. At noon the Y.W.C.A. Orchestra was replaced by the Larkin String Orchestra which had already made a name for itself with its weekly radio broadcasts. Again under the direction of Mr. Ball, and with W. M. Isham, the composer, at the piano, they played "My Fifty Golden Years" written especially for the occasion.

At sometime after 1:00 the reception in the office was concluded. There is no further account of the events of that day in the record. John must have been tired after the long hours of greeting employees and friends. Perhaps he was able to relax over lunch with the directors and members of his family who were with him and to take a short nap on the couch in his office, as was his custom. In the afternoon there would have been business to tend to. Hundreds of telegrams and letters of congratulation needed to be sorted and read with the help of members of the President's Office staff, and some matters of business that could not wait required attention as usual.

The day passed quickly and happily. When Charles Pratt came at 4:30 to drive him home, John was ready. He was tired, but filled with a sense of accomplishment. He had worked hard during his 80 years and always with the vision of creating something that would benefit those he loved, his family and his fellow human beings. This day had celebrated the success of that vision. His family was provided for, and he had performed some service for humanity.

John's life had not always been an easy one. He had gone to work early to help support his widowed mother, and he had known physical labor, long hours and apparent failure. The thought of retirement would probably never have occurred to him. There had been many disappointments in his life, all of which he met with the same quiet faith. He was not a man who wore his religion on his sleeve, but in a very deep sense he was religious. To the end of his life he supported the Baptist church into which he had been born, although he was no longer an active member of any congregation. It would be accurate to say that John was a Christian in the truest and best sense of the word.

The story of John D. Larkin's life is worth telling both for itself and for its place in American social and business history. The cast of characters will include such well known names as Elbert Hubbard, Frank Lloyd Wright, Darwin D. Martin, Mrs. Grover Cleveland, Paderewski, Billy Sunday and King Albert I of Belgium, as well has a host of ordinary Americans for whom the name Larkin became a household word. To tell the story of John D. Larkin we need to go back to its beginning in the little town of Beckley, in Kent, England, where John's father, Levi H. Larkin, was born.

---

[1] I have known and talked with many former employees over the years, and all have spoken of John Larkin with respect and affection.

[2] *Buffalo Courier Express*, February 16, 1926, p. 1. Anecdote recounted by John D. Larkin Jr.

[3] *Ourselves*, May 8, 1925, p. 1, Buffalo and Erie County Historical Society, hereinafter referred to as BECHS.

[4] Ibid.

Chapter 1

English Roots

Levi Henry Larkin, the father of John D. Larkin, was the youngest of ten children born to Henry and Hannah Catt Larkin. The Larkins lived in the little town of Beckley, a few miles north and west of Rye, in the county of Sussex, England. Young Levi was born May 23, 1817. He spent his boyhood in the village, attended school there, undoubtedly helped with the hop harvest and probably spent some time as apprentice to a blacksmith.

When Levi Larkin was born, his oldest brother, George, was already twenty four. Henry, Susan and James were young adults making their way in the world. William, seventeen years older than Levi, went to America around 1821 to seek his fortune, returning to England some years later. Levi's sister, Mary, was just ten years older, and with her younger sister, Harriet, must have been a great help to Hannah in the care of their baby brother. In 1821, Mary and Edmund Ralph (then spelled Ralf) were married in the little church in the neighboring village of Etchingham.[1]

Edmund's family had a brickyard near East Grinstead in Surrey which supplied brick for the building of the oast houses used in the curing of hops. The Ralphs were reasonably prosperous, but like so many others they were lured by reports of opportunities in the new world. When Levi was twelve years old, his sister Mary and her husband left Rye for America, perhaps encouraged by William's accounts of success in the new world. Levi was to follow them five years later.

Very little is known about Levi's parents. Was Henry a farmer? His wife Hannah wrote to Mary in October of 1834, "There has been a great many hops grown in Sussex this year—11 months and five weeks hoping [sic] and fine weather." That they knew at least a modest degree of prosperity is suggested by Hannah's reference in her letter to "Samuel the gardener (sic)." The Larkin children had the basic schooling that would have been available to them in an English village, but undoubtedly the greatest emphasis in their upbringing would have been religious.

Henry and Hannah were not Church of England, but adhered to the strict tenets of the Baptist faith. Hannah Catt's letters to Mary reflect a deeply religious spirit, and, when Levi left for America in 1834, she placed in his hands a book entitled *The Whole Duty Of Man Or, The Christian's Companion* by the Rev. Charles Atmore, to be a guide for the salvation of her son's soul.[2] The book sets forth the basic Christian scheme of Creation, Transgression and Salvation with heavy emphasis on the transitory nature of earthly life and the necessity of preparing for an eternity which will consist either of bliss or damnation according to one's conduct on earth. There is much emphasis on such matters as "carefulness to save the soul," "the depravity of man," and "the carnal mind in enmity against God." Strong stuff for a boy of seventeen and guaranteed to keep him on the straight and narrow when the alternative is hellfire and eternal damnation.

It is not irrelevant to note here that this kind of strict Protestantism flourished in England during the reigns of the the sons of George III—the Prince Regent, who became George IV in 1820—and William IV, known as "Silly Billy," who reigned from 1830 until the accession of Queen Victoria in 1837. It was a period of gross excesses on the part of the privileged classes and of cruel oppression of the "lower orders." In addition to the political and moral chaos of the period, the accelerating industrial revolution was creating havoc with the social fabric of England.

Making a living was not easy in Kent and Sussex in the early 19th Century. The iron industry of the Kentish Weald, which had been a source of great wealth and prosperity in the 16th and 17th centuries, had declined almost to extinction by the end of the 18th Century. One of the Cinque Ports under Richard I, Rye had been a thriving port until the sea receded and the rivers that surround the town had filled with silt. Rye had died as a major port long before Levi took ship for America. While it was still an active port, its rivers were too shallow to accommodate anything but small craft. Hops had replaced iron and shipping as the mainstay of the area's economy, and for many the going was hard.

No wonder, then, that the children of Henry and Hannah Larkin sought to improve their lives by a move to the new frontier on the other side of the Atlantic. Dates and practice signatures in the front of *The Whole Duty Of Man*, the book Levi brought to America, suggest that William may have carried the same book with him as early as 1821. Hannah speaks in her letters to Mary of the hope that "if the Lord is pleased to spare his life and mine a few years he [Levi] may be able to come to England once more as William has done."

For all its promise, the move was not an easy one. Mary and Edmund Ralph and their three children sailed for America on Sunday, May 16, 1829, on the ship *Ulysses* of Baltimore.[3] For the next six weeks the travelers endured the crowded discomfort of an Atlantic packet and the misery of a rough passage. They landed in New York on Sunday June 27th, six weeks to the day from their last glimpse of Old England. But the journey was far from over. From New York, they traveled by canal boat up the Hudson and then by the newly opened Erie Canal to Buffalo. They were in Schenectady on the 4th of July, and finally reached Buffalo on July 17th. It was a long and tiring journey for a young mother with two girls, aged six and three, and a baby boy in her arms.

Edmund's plan was to board a boat that would take them to Cleveland and then proceed overland to Pittsburgh, but this was not to be. There are several versions of Mary and Edmund Ralph's decision to stay in Buffalo. One version states that Mary, weary of the trials of boat travel, simply put her foot down and refused to board another ship. A second version reports that the sailing to Cleveland was delayed by adverse winds. While the packet waited for a favorable wind, Edmund set out to look over the village of Buffalo. In the course of his tour, he was engaged in conversation by Deacon Goodell, who, when he discovered that Ralph was skilled in the art of brickmaking, urged the young man to consider settling in Buffalo. The village needed a brickyard, and as the good Deacon was anxious to build a substantial brick house for himself, he offered Ralph a log house on the corner of Main Street and a country lane called Goodell. Opposite stood the imposing mansion of Judge Ebenezer Waldon with its Greek revival facade. The prospect of ending the voyage then and there and settling down to make a living was irresistible. Mary and Edmund gathered up their children and belongings and moved into the Deacon's log house. Edmund Ralph records that the Ralphs lived in the front and Deacon Jabez Goodell in the balance of the house. "Mr. Ralph rented a parcel of land lying between Virginia Street and Burton Alley and extending east from Elm Street for several acres. . . Mr. Ralph ultimately bought this tract of land and built a house at No. 313 Elm Street."[4]

The Ralphs remained in Buffalo and prospered in the brick business until the dreadful epidemic of cholera in the summer of 1832. In June of that year, their daughter Mary, aged 9, succumbed to the disease. Some weeks later, Edmund was stricken and died on August 27. Mary was a widow with three children at the age of twenty six. As if that were not burden enough, Edmund's sister, Elizabeth Hilder, her husband and a large family had arrived in Buffalo from England about August 1st. They had barely begun to settle into their new home with Edmund and Mary when the plague struck, and of their entire family only two children survived. Mary assumed the care of the survivors, little Ann and Jerry Hilder.[5] In spite of her dreadful losses, and the care of five children, the widow Ralph managed to carry on the business of the brickyard with considerable success.

Perhaps influenced by Mary's plight, Levi decided in 1834 to make the trip to America and join his sister in Buffalo. Mr. Allard, who had worked for Edmund Ralph in his brickyard, had come to England to marry his fiancee and bring her back to Buffalo. In early April of 1834, Levi together with the Allards set sail for America. It must have been a rough passage, for Hannah wrote to Mary after receiving news of her son's safe arrival, "I was sorry to hear he was so ill on the passage but thankfull to kind Providence for having provided a remedy. It was my wish for him to have taken some Tincture of Rhubarb with him. I am very happy he is so comfortable and that he goes to a Sunday School and I sincerely hope he will live in the fear of the Lord and then there is no doubt but he will do well."[6]

How welcome must have been the day when Mary saw her young brother and Mr. and Mrs. Allard step off the canal boat that had brought them the last leg of the long journey from England. Hannah's letter suggests that the lad soon forgot the rigors of the Atlantic crossing in the excitement and promise of his new home. The seventeen year old Levi would have found Mary's home a lively place. The children, Tamar, 8, Edmund, 6 and Reuben, 4, were delighted with their new found cousin. His sea sickness soon forgotten, he thrilled them with tales of life on shipboard and entered into their games. They were allowed to go with him to show him the new and teeming harbor and to watch the comings and goings of ships sailing past the proud stone lighthouse at its entrance. It was a time when Buffalo was caught up in the great wave of western emigration and the mania for land speculation that would burst like a bubble in the economic collapse of the panic of 1837. In the five years between 1830 and 1835, the population of Buffalo jumped from 8,668 to 15,661. The village that became a chartered city in 1832 was the gateway to the west, and from her harbor thousands of hopeful emigrants set sail to fulfill the dream of a prosperous new life. By 1837 forty-two steamboats were busy on Lake Erie ferrying this flood of humanity westward.

Levi must have been reminded of Rye by this river harbor that looked out on the vast expanse of water, but the differences between the two cities would have outweighed any similarities. Here everything was new and spacious. Families lived, for the most part, in separate houses, and the houses occupied spacious lots.[7] Many dwellings were of log construction, but there were already porticoed mansions like that of Judge Walden. Edmund Ralph's brick factory had made possible the added luxury of building with brick. The Rev. Dr. Hosmer, who came to Buffalo in 1836, gives the following description of the streets. "Main Street was as broad as Mr. Ellicott laid it out, but its mud was said to have no bottom. I have seen teams sloughed on Mohawk Street, near Delaware . . . I saw a young lady one day sloughed in the middle of Pearl Street, near Tupper, so that she could not step without leaving behind her shoes and overshoes, perhaps the whole foot apparel, and there she stood with a patience peculiar to those days, until I got boards and made a way for her poor feet."[8] Mrs. Martha Fitch Poole gives a vivid picture of Buffalo in 1835. "Indians walked the street in blankets and moccasins, cows were grazing at the roadsides, and pigs roamed at their own sweet will, only kept out of beautiful gardens by stout fences, usually of the picket variety. Yet Buffalo was a very beautiful city, notwithstanding." Mrs. Poole goes on to extol the virtues of Mr. Ellicott's elegant plan, the stately trees that lined the streets, and the uninterrupted views of lake and river. "Buffalo was a bustling business place eight months of the year, say from April to December. The other four were given up quite generally to social enjoyment."[9]

Social enjoyment for Levi and his sister's family would have had its center in the Baptist church located at the corner of Washington and Seneca Streets. We know from her mother's letter that Mary had reported that Levi was attending Sunday school. The Larkins and the Ralphs were deeply religious and strict followers of the tenets of the Baptist Church. Their Sundays, and many hours of their weekdays, would have been spent in the company of their fellow parishioners. On Sunday the sermon, anywhere from one to two hours in length, was the centerpiece of the service, dealing chiefly with the doctrines of the church, salvation, hellfire and the Day of Judgment. Mary Hubbard Heath remembers the terror similar sermons inspired in her as a little girl. "I listened with horror, waiting for certain inevitable passages describing the Judgment Day. . . the scenes of Gabriel coming in the clouds of Heaven, the blast of his trumpet, the separation of the sheep from the goats, and the awful sentence to the left hand of the throne of God."[10] Hymns with such lines as "Hark, from the tombs a doleful sound" did nothing to cheer the terrified child. After the New Year, the visiting evangelists came on their rounds and classes would be held for the conversion of young people and adults not yet baptized. For those who could finally answer correctly the questions put to them by the Deacons, the next step was the baptism itself, the total immersion, often in the icy waters of a nearby creek. The Washington Street Baptist Church, at the corner of Seneca and Washington Streets, and the Cottage Baptist Church at Clinton and Washington streets served as gathering places for families of like persuasion, centers of the family social life.

How long Levi may have lived with his sister, we can only guess. It is certain that her situation changed considerably when an old friend of the Ralphs', Philo A. Balcom, came in from Hamburg to assist the widow with the brickyard. Philo was a man of considerable experience with many connections in the community. His stepson, Edmund S. Ralph, records that he had been in charge of the toll bridge across Buffalo Creek, and that he "was boss in building the Hamburg Turnpike for O.H. Dibble in 1833—he also had run the ferry boat [across] the Creek for Mr. S. Pratt, Father of Samuel F. and Pascal P. Pratt. . ."[11] Mary Ralph and Philo A. Balcom were married November 27, 1837, prospered in the brick business, and added to the family four children of their own. In the same journal entry, Edmund Ralph notes that on June 20, 1837, "Victoria succeeded to the throne of England as Queen." A new era had begun.

Levi Larkin had served his apprenticeship to a blacksmith in England and had acquired considerable skill in the mysteries of the forge. He hadn't been long in Buffalo when he met George Jones and was offered work in Jones' "iron works." There is no record of when he started with Jones, but in the Buffalo City Directories of 1838—1840 Levi is listed as "blacksmith with George Jones," and it seems reasonable to assume that their association probably began shortly after Levi arrived in Buffalo.

By the time his sister remarried, Levi had established himself as an active member of the burgeoning community. His friend and employer, George Jones, held the position of Chief Engineer in the old Volunteer Fire Department, and Levi soon joined as a member of the Eagle Hose Company.[12] Through George Jones and Mary and Philo Balcom, he must have made valuable contacts in the growing business community. With Mary and her family he attended the Washington Street Baptist Church and participated in the social life of the community. Perhaps at some church social, he met a pretty girl who had come with friends from Winterbourne, Ontario, near Guelph. To say that she "came" to Buffalo (as one might today by bus or train) is a real understatement. She and her friends had walked the hundred miles and thought nothing of it.

Mary Ann Durrant, like Levi, had been born in England. Her parents had left their home in Kent in 1831, when Mary was twelve years old. The homestead that they established near Guelph, Ontario, proved to be equal to their expectations, and the family continued to farm there for over a hundred years. With their mutual English backgrounds, it is little wonder that the two young people were drawn to each other. Whether Mary Ann returned to Winterbourne on foot and then returned again to marry Levi is not recorded. In any event, they were married on the 29th of December, 1838, probably in either the Washington Street Baptist Church, at the corner of Seneca and Swan Streets, or in the newly formed Cottage Baptist Church farther uptown at Washington and Clinton Streets. The marriage certificate was witnessed by George Jones and another friend, G. D. Crocker.

Levi apparently continued to work with George Jones until 1841, when he is no longer listed with Jones in the City Directory. He and Mary moved several times between 1838 and 1844, and the Directory for 1842 lists "Larkin, Levi H. blacksmith main c[orner] chippewa." By 1844 the young couple with their three children had moved to No. 13 Clinton Street. Levi was in business for himself and doing well enough to have his own business card:

> LEVI H. LARKIN / MANUFACTURER OF / IRON FENCE, / STAIR RAILING, WINDOW SHUTTERS / AND HOUSE SMITHING IN GENERAL, / No. 13, Clinton Street, / In the rear of the Cottage Baptist Church. / Buffalo, N.Y.

Levi Larkin prospered. He soon hired Robert M. Bingham and several other men to help with the growing volume of business. By 1852, Bingham is listed as "Foreman L.H. Larkin" in the City Directory. The ledger in which Levi kept the record of his business at No. 13 Clinton Street between 1849 and 1852 can be found in the Rare Book Room of the Buffalo and Erie County Public Library. Its many entries suggest a lively trade in everything from sash weights to verandah railings and chimney irons. In addition to the various aspects of smithing, the ledger suggests that Levi was engaged as well in the cleaning and repairing of clocks. The list of customers includes many names familiar in the annals of Buffalo: Balcom, Blossom, Coit, Case, Dodge, Fargo, Gates, Hodge, Hayes, Jewett and Ketchum, among others. That his former employer George Jones appears in a number of entries suggests that their relationship remained a friendly one, and we can be sure that their interests in the church and in the Fire Department remained a continuing bond between the two men. For a young man with a growing family, Levi was doing very well.

On September 29, 1845, a baby boy was born at No. 13 Clinton Street, and Mary and Levi named him John Durrant. His older siblings, Mary Ann, born September 13, 1843; Levi H., born September 17, 1841, and Hannah Catt, born October 29, 1839, must have been delighted with the new arrival, and we know that members of the Cottage Baptist Church, including Juliana Frances Read (John's future mother-in-law) lost no time in calling to congratulate the proud parents.[13] When John was two years old, a brother, Alvin James was born on September 30, 1847, and he was followed in a few years by William George (February 20, 1850) and Harriet Sarah (April 3, 1852). Levi proudly recorded these births in the Family Bible which he acquired in 1846, shortly after John's arrival. Many years later, his son John had the old book repaired, its binding redone, and the name LARKIN placed on the front cover in gold block letters by the Buffalo bookbinder John F. Grabau. A sheet pasted into the repaired book bearing the name Levi Henry Larkin and dated Buffalo, January 1846 appears to be in Levi's hand. This Bible is now in the Rare Books collection of the Buffalo and Erie County Public Library, located directly opposite the site of Levi's home and forge at 13 Clinton Street.

When little John was only four, an event occurred which he later spoke of as one of his earliest recollections, the burning of the old Eagle Tavern. At 5 o'clock on the morning of November 14, 1849, the fire alarm bells rang out. One can imagine the commotion in the house on Clinton Street as Levi scrambled out of bed, pulled on his clothes and rushed to his station with the Volunteer Fire Department. He was followed, no doubt, by the older children as the town turned out to see the conflagration. The Eagle Tavern and its block of tenements was already engulfed in a raging fire. The alarm bells had been sounded late, and the firemen found themselves at a considerable disadvantage from a lack of water. The *Buffalo Daily Courier* reported next day that "such was the combustible character of the old tenement that the whole of the rear side of the court was soon destroyed and the flames had communicated to the wooden part on Main Street, as well as to the brick building known as the Tavern proper." The paper praised the firemen for their usual bravery and noted that "one or more firemen were injured, by falling from a ladder into a bed of hot ashes."[14]

The great fire threatened other buildings in the area, and John recalled that his father distinguished himself by an act of considerable daring. Someone discovered that sparks from the blazing tavern had lodged in the belfry of the old Court House on Washington Street. A cry went up that the building was in imminent danger, and there was great concern, for no water could reach the spot. Levi and a group of firemen ran to the rescue. Levi was first up the ladder and managed to scale the slippery shingles and extinguish the fire with his coat. The old Court House was saved. As the building stood directly across Clinton Street from Levi's home, Mary Ann and little John may well have watched this daring act from their own front door. What excitement there must have been when the family assembled again at 13 Clinton Street to welcome their hero home!

Mary Ann must have felt some anxiety about her husband's willingness to expose himself to danger in the pursuit of his duty as a fireman. If so, she may have had reason to be apprehensive. Only two years later, Levi contracted pneumonia after fighting a particularly stubborn fire. He was exhausted from his efforts and on June 27, 1852, after a brief illness, he died at the age of 35, only three months after the birth of his youngest daughter. Mary Ann was left a widow at the age of 33, with seven children to care for ranging in age from three months to thirteen years.

At the time of his death in 1852, Levi's personal property was appraised at $147.00 (including the family Bible), with $300.00 cash on hand and a business inventory of $1,902.25. The property at No. 13 Clinton St. was held under a mortgage in the amount of $1,650.00 payable to Ira A. Blossom to come due on April 8, 1856, with interest payable semi-annually. In 1855, Mary Ann Larkin and Douglas M. Williams, administrators of Levi's estate under letters of administration granted by the surrogate of the County of Erie on July 13, 1852, estimated the value of the Clinton Street real estate to be "about eight thousand dollars in the judgment of your Petitioners."[15] Mary left No. 13 Clinton St. shortly after her husband's death and life was never the same again for John and his brothers and sisters.

---

[1] Edmund S. Ralph, *Chronicles of our Family*, 1894 MS, copy given to me by Dorothy L. Ralph.

[2] Levi Larkin's copy of this book is in the Rare Book Room of the Buffalo and Erie County Public Library.

[3] Ralph, *Chronicles*, 1829.

[4] Grace Carew Sheldon, "The Balcom Homestead," *The Buffalo Evening Times*, Saturday, April 24, 1909, p.4.

[5] Ralph, *Chronicles*, 1832.

[6] Hannah Larkin, letter to Mary Ralph, dated Beckley, October 31, 1834, typed copy in author's collection.

[7] J.N. Larned, *A History of Buffalo*, New York: The Progress of the Empire State Company, 1911, Vol I, p.144.

[8] Larned, I, p.142.

[9] Larned, I, p.55.

[10] Mary Hubbard Heath, *The Elbert Hubbard I Knew*, East Aurora, N.Y.: The Roycrofters, 1929, p. 126.

[11] Ralph, *Chronicles*, 1837.

[12] Milton G. Wolfe, *Jones Iron Works 1815-1941*, privately published, 1981, p. 4; *Memorial and Family History of Erie County, New York*, New York–Buffalo: The Genealogical Publishing Company, 1906-8.

[13] Mary Hubbard Heath, *The Elbert Hubbard I Knew*, p. 147.

[14] *Buffalo Daily Courier*, "Local Matters, &c." November 15, 1849.

[15] Petition on file with the Surrogate Court of the County of Erie to sell property in the estate of Levi H. Larkin at 13 Clinton Street, dated July 18, 1855.

Chapter 2

The Early Years

The years following Levi Larkin's death were difficult ones for his widow Mary. Their seven children ranged in age from Hannah, who was thirteen, to little Harriet, only two months old. Seven year old John stood squarely in the middle. Mary was fortunate in having Robert Bingham, Levi's foreman in the iron works at 13 Clinton Street, to run the business. Eventually Bingham assumed the ownership of the works and after several moves established his own business, the Clinton Iron Works, at the "corner Church and Jackson Sts., near Gas Works."[1]

Mary moved out of the Clinton Street house shortly after her husband's death, first to 203 Oak Street, and then to "Elm north of Virginia."[2] The Elm Street property may well have belonged to her brother-in-law Philo Balcom, who had by that date moved to Cold Spring and built a fine home at the corner of Main and Ferry. It would have been natural for Levi's sister Mary to extend every help and support she could to his widow and her family. The families were close, and as John grew up he would always have the affectionate concern of "Auntie Balcom" and the friendship of the Ralph and Balcom cousins.

Mary Larkin, however, was a strong and independent woman and from the start she managed her affairs well. She had made arrangements for Levi's burial in the old North Street Cemetery. In 1853, probably at the suggestion of Philo Balcom, she purchased a lot in the recently opened Forest Lawn Cemetery, and Levi's body was moved there. The year 1855, when John was just 10, must have been a particularly difficult one for Mary. In April she lost her little Harriet, just three years old, to whooping cough. The property at 13 Clinton Street was becoming a burden. What arrangements she made with Robert Bingham are not known, but the mortgage on the property in the amount of $1,650 plus interest, held by Ira Blossom would become due in April of 1856. Mary, and Douglas W. Williams, administrators of Levi Larkin's estate, petitioned the Surrogate Court of Erie County for permission to sell the Clinton Street property, and Alfred W. Wilgus was appointed "special guardian" to represent the interests of the children in the settlement of the real estate proceedings.

The property was finally offered for sale in the spring of 1856, and Mary must have felt a great relief when it was finally sold to Daniel S. Forbes and Stephen M. Newton for $2,898.78.[3]

The year 1856 would be John's last year attending Buffalo's Public School #15. Although there is evidence that Mary found work as a nurse,[4] evidently what she was able to earn was not enough to meet the needs of six growing children. Levi and John both had to pitch in and help, and the record states that John first went to work at the age of twelve as a messenger boy for the Western Union Telegraph Company.[5] He may even have started in this work before the end of the school year, but he was not to remain long as a messenger boy. Probably before the end of the year, John was hired by Mr. William H. Woodward, a milliner whose fashionable emporium was located at 287–289 Main Street at the corner of Eagle. In his advertisement in the City Directory for 1860, Woodward presents himself as "Wholesale and Retail Dealer in Straw Goods, Artificial Flowers, Ribbons, Silks, Satins, Velvets, and Millinery Articles." John may have started as a delivery boy, but his quiet, steady disposition and his strict attention to business would have recommended him strongly to his employer, and it is probable that he soon rose to stockboy and eventually clerk. He had a good head for figures, was keenly observant of the world around him and related sensitively to others. Added to these qualities, he was a handsome boy and possessed a sense of fun that could add a light touch to a serious matter of fashion. He was undoubtedly a favorite among the ladies who patronized Mr. Woodward's emporium. Here the lad would have had his first taste of business and his first glimpse into the fashionable world of Buffalo's wealthier families.

John continued to work for Woodward for the next four years, until a new direction was opened to him in 1861 by the marriage of his sister Mary to Justus Weller. Weller was an enterprising young man, handsome and full of fun, who had opened a soap factory on Seneca Street north of the N.Y. & Erie R.R. crossing.[6] His business was small but prospering, and the home that he and Mary made became a second home to John. Weller took his brother-in-law on as a clerk and general assistant, and from the evidence in the diaries we know that John lived with Jus and Mary on and off over the next ten years. However, the picture, as presented in the official accounts issued during his lifetime, of John working for Weller consistently over the years until their removal to Chicago in 1870 is inaccurate. From the diaries which he kept in 1865, 1867 and 1869, it is clear that during these years young John was unsettled, trying to find himself, exploring various possibilities.

The years between 1861, when John first worked for Jus Weller, and 1865, the year of the first diary, were turbulant times for the nation, and enthusiasm ran high in the city for the new Republican party and its anti-slavery platform. On the afternoon of February 16, 1861, President-elect Abraham Lincoln stopped in Buffalo on his way to Washington to assume the leadership of the nation, and almost certainly John, with his brother Levi and Jus, was part of the vast crowd that turned out to welcome him. His reception by the crowd at the railroad station was "so tumultously enthusiastic and ill-controlled that he and his party were nearly crushed."[7] It may be hard to imagine the quiet, dignified John D. Larkin of later years involved in such a melee, but John was only sixteen at the time and feelings run high when one is young and principles are at stake. John Larkin was a staunch Republican for the rest of his life. The Southern Confederacy had already been formed, and on April 12, the bombardment of Fort Sumter signaled the beginning of the Civil War. Buffalo, with a population of over 81,000, would send hundreds of her young men into the dreadful conflict. John Larkin was young and a vital link in the support of his mother and younger siblings. There is no record of his ever being involved in the military.

1865 was an eventful year for John. Sometime in the previous year he had enrolled as a student in Bryant and Stratton business school, which had opened its doors in Buffalo in 1854. John gives no details of the nature of the course that he took; however, Darwin D. Martin, writing in 1882, describes the six month's course that he will enroll in as consisting of "writing, double and single entry bookkeeping" at a cost of $25 to $30. The course that John took was probably the same.[8] Undoubtedly Jus had encouraged him in this. An employee trained in business methods would be an asset in the growing business. In addition, Jus had a scheme in mind in which he would use John to manage a kind of branch business to sell soap in New York and Brooklyn. Weller's sister Jennie was married to Thomas J. Preston, owner of Thomas J. Preston & Co., Linseed Crushers, 80 River Street, Newark, NJ. What better idea than to send John to New York where he could live with the Prestons and establish a base from which to distribute Weller's soap in the New York-Brooklyn area.

Entries in John's diary for the first two weeks of January, 1865, give interesting glimpses of his day-to-day life:

> *Sunday, January 1, 1865, Went to church morning and evening. Commenced storming this evening, wind blows quite hard.*
>
> *Monday January 2 Went Skating this morning. This afternoon went up town. Went to Mother's to tea.*
>
> *Tuesday January 3 Went to School this Morning This afternoon Commenced working in Large Books.*
>
> *Friday January 6, Worked in the Factory this Morning. went to School this afternoon and Evening. Recd my Scholarship today.*
>
> *Saturday, January 7, Took out a load of S.[oft] Soap today. it is very cold. Went Sleigh Riding this Evening had a very Pleasant time.*
>
> *Sunday, January 8, Went to Church morning and evening. Took charge of a class in Sunday School today*
>
> *Monday, January 9 Went to School this Morning afternoon and Evening. It is snowing.*
>
> *Tuesday, January 10 Got a load of Fleshings this morning. worked in the Factory all the afternoon. It has been snowing all day. The wind is blowing very hard*
>
> *Wednesday, January 11, got up at 5A.M. run the tank worked at home all day. Sat up and run the tank till 2 O'clock. Still Storming very hard.*
>
> *Thursday, January 12, got up at 9 ½ A.M. worked at home till 4 O'clock then cleaned up and went up town. It has cleared up pleasant. Wind blows a little*
>
> *Friday, January 13 Went to school all day. Carried my books home. Called to see mother then went home and staid all the evening. The weather is quite pleasant*
>
> *Saturday, January 14 Storming rather hard. Took out a load of S Soap and Some hard Soap. Tonight I watch with Mr Laycock who died this morning*
>
> *Sunday, January 15 Went to bed at 8 ½ got up at 11 ½ O'clock Went to S. School with Pony and Cutter. Went home. Took Aggie over with me. Tonight Jus and I start for New York at 6 O'clock*

The trip to New York was undoubtedly John's first, and between the lines of his quiet, matter-of-fact entries we catch a glimpse of an observant young man who enjoyed life and participated fully in it. The two men arrived in New York at 2 o'clock on the afternoon of January 16, and arrived at the Prestons' "a little before dark." John is never specific about locations, but the evidence seems to suggest that the Prestons lived somewhere in the Brooklyn area.[9] In the four days that he was with the Prestons, John seems to have left most of the business arrangements to Jus while he took in the sights of the big city. On Wednesday the 18th, he notes a visit to Wall Street, to a sugar refinery, to Ball and Black's jewelers, and to the Barnum Museum. "Had a fine time. Weather very Cold." Thursday was devoted to business, but Friday afternoon he "went to the Gold Room then to Central Park and Skated 1 hour then went to see Weller." Saturday they left for home at 7:30 in the morning, and, after delays at Troy and Syracuse, arrived home in Buffalo at 10:30 Sunday morning.

During the months of February and March John devoted most of his time to completing his courses at Bryant & Stratton and then to making preparations for the New York venture. Weekdays were almost wholly spent at school. Saturdays he worked in the Factory tending "the Patent Soap Maker" or cutting soap. Some Saturdays he went uptown "collecting" or "looking for ashes." Sundays were devoted to church and Sunday school and social gatherings. On March 14, John completed his schooling. He stayed with his mother on the 15th, and the entry for the 16th reads: "went to school all day in the afternoon carried my books home it is storming got a letter from Levi today."

Mary must have been very proud of her son that day. His brother Levi never seemed to settle down or complete anything, but John's steady pursuit of whatever goal he set himself showed great promise for the future. Jus, too, must have been pleased with his brother-in-law, and confident that the New York venture would be a success.

March brought its usual roller coaster weather to Buffalo with alternating warm and cold, wind and rain. . There was severe flooding "east and down the river." John was working full time now for Jus, tending to the soap, or collecting uptown. He was busy, too, drawing up the partnership agreement that he had worked out with Jus. The document seems to be in John's hand and may well display the first results of his recent schooling. The men agreed "to be co-partners together under the firm name of Larkin & Weller in the business of making/selling Soft Soap in the Cities of New York and Brooklyn and elsewhere."

They bought a wagon to be used for delivery in the New York and Brooklyn area, and, on March 28, John went out to Lancaster to pick it up. He spent the next two days painting the wagon the green that he and Jus favored and applying the firm name Larkin & Weller in handsome black letters trimmed with red.

On April 4th, John records: "got all the things to the Depot today." The stock of soap and the wagon went by freight, and on April 6th Jus left for New York. John followed on the 8th, after making several trips uptown to "bid Mother and Hannah Goodbye." He arrived in Jersey City at 6 o'clock on the morning of Monday, the 10th of April, and went over to Greenpoint in the rain. After several days of waiting, the supplies arrived in New York, John had them carted to Greenpoint, and Jus picked up the wagon and hard soap. Larkin & Weller were ready to launch their business, and John entered in the ledger which he kept over a period of years the "Inventory of Property owned by Larkin & Weller:

One Horse	171.00
Wagon and Frame	107.75
Harness	27.00
Two pails	9.00
One dipper	2.75
Steam Pipes	10.69"[10]

Selling was slow at first. Saturday, April 15, "Today we took a load over to N.Y. Brought most of it back again. Sold all of the hard soap. Lincoln died this morning from a pistol shot." The shock of Lincoln's assassination virtually brought business to a halt. On the following Monday, John went to Hastings on an outing with the Prestons. "Had a very pleasant time. We went up on the Palisades." He made several trips to York for ashes in the next few days, but for the most part stayed "home" with the Prestons. Although he makes no mention of it in the diary, he must have been occupied making the soft soap that he was to sell in the area. On Friday, April 21, he paid $1.10 for four fish barrels which he may have used to transport the liquid soap, and received letters from Levi and Mary. He went to church twice on Sunday as usual and "wrote a letter to Mother." Jus had returned to Buffalo the week before, and John was on his own now to manage his end of the business.

On Monday, April 24, the young soap manufacturer loaded his wagon and set out to sell soft soap in Brooklyn. He went to [New] York after business cards he had ordered that the ledger says cost him $4.00, and the diary records that on that day Lincoln's body arrived in New York. The city gave itself over to an elaborate expression of grief. The next day, Tuesday, April 25, 1865, no business was transacted, and John's entry in the diary is brief, but expressive: "Went over to New York to see the President's funeral procession it was the largest I ever see" The youth from Buffalo shared with the thousands who lined the streets of New York that day the deep sense of loss that Whitman turned to music in his great poem "When Lilacs Last in the Dooryard Bloomed."

The weeks that followed were not easy ones for John: selling soap was often discouraging work. The diary entry for May 4, 1865, is characteristic: "Went to Brooklyn with Soft Soap it is hard work to sell it." The diary suggests that John made the soft soap at Greenpoint, and the ledger seems to bear this out, but that the hard soap was shipped to him from Buffalo. The ledger indicates that grease and ashes were cheap: grease @7 cents a pound, and ashes for the hauling. The soft soap was sold by the gallon—18 ½ cents per gal., ten gallons $1.87. Interestingly, the soap was frequently paid for in grease or a combination of cash and grease. Typical sales ran from one to ten gallons, with occasional sales of one barrel at $6.00 per bbl.

Except for the few entries in which John records that the selling of soft soap was difficult, it is significant that John never even mentions the physical labor involved in what he was doing. Boiling soap was a smelly, nasty business, and the hard physical labor involved in hauling and handling both the raw materials and the finished product had to be considerable. Yet through June, July and August the most frequent entry reads simply "Went to Brooklyn with Soft soap." Some days he stays home because of rain, at other times the weather catches him out and he gets "wet through." On the 9th of June, Levi came to join him, and they went together to Brooklyn with soft soap the next day. Apparently the drudgery of selling soap did not appeal to Levi, and there is no further record of his accompanying his brother on his rounds. Instead he did some work for Mr. Preston and a month later returned to Buffalo. Indeed, in later years when John was a highly successful businessman, he would try repeatedly to settle Levi in some aspect of the business, but it would never last more than a few days or weeks. Levi did go to work for Mr. Preston, but after a month he quit. The difference between the two brothers was dramatic: the one tenacious, uncomplaining, with a cheerful tolerance for drudgery, if it led to a desired goal; the other sorely lacking in the self-discipline that might lead him to success. Nevertheless John was glad to have his brother with him to share his life with the Prestons and his exploration of the world around New York.

Life was not all work and no play, and one side of John was as full of fun as the other was of business. There was church on Sundays, often twice, as important a social event as it was a religious one. There were the young Prestons, Thomas and "the babies," to enjoy outings with. There were excursions to Coney Island, to New Rochelle, and one to Keyport and around Staten Island during which the Prestons' house was robbed while they were out. Mr. Preston may have owned property in Hasting, and there are numerous references to the children's spending time there. A friend, Frank Hull, came from Buffalo to visit in June, and, in July, John went to hear Henry Ward Beecher speak. On the day that Levi quit his job with Mr. Preston, John made an excursion to the Navy Yard. The next day, July 19, he "went over to N.Y. and then went down to Cony [sic] Island with Levi." On Thursday the brothers were in New York again, and the entry in the diary gives an interesting insight into John's characteristic attention to detail. "Went to the Trinity Church whose steeple is 284 feet high, then went out to Central Park which covers 850 acres one lake has 25 acres one 20 one 5 one 3 one 2 and one 1 acre. Had our Phiz taken in the cave." The next day, Friday, John took hard soap into New York, and at six o'clock that evening he and Levi started for Buffalo.

The journey to Buffalo was uneventful. They took the river boat up the Hudson to Albany, arriving "about daylight," and then boarded "the Cars" at 8:45 and arrived in Buffalo at 9:00 that night. "They were very much surprised to see us. Stayed at Justus's tonight." The next day was Sunday and there was church morning and evening. John "staid to Sunday school. It seems just like home. Stay at Mother's tonight." He divided his time for the next five days between "home" with Jus and Mary and "uptown" with his mother. There was tea every day with Mary and Hannah, his mother and friends. A choir rehearsal was held at Jus' house Tuesday evening, on Wednesday he visited the Ralphs and Balcoms in Cold Springs, and the Cedar Street picnic at Alden was the highlight on Thursday. Of the picnic he writes: "Had quite a nice time. We all went up and had some ice cream in the evening." Friday John spent the day with Jus, took tea with his mother and left for New York at 10:40, in the rain. The train arrived in Albany at 9:40 the next morning, and John took the day boat for New York. "Was on the Hudson untill 6:25 got over home at 8 o'clock."

Back with the Prestons life resumed its previous patterns, but with a difference. Doing the rounds of Brooklyn with soft soap occupied most days, but often he would stay home, work on the books, or do work for Mr. Preston. In early August young Tom and Jennie Preston went to visit in Buffalo, and John took them to the boat that would take them up the Hudson to Albany. In mid August he was sick, and after that he seems to make fewer trips to Brooklyn, staying home, helping Jennie put up her fruit or going with her to market, driving for the Prestons or going out for a load of hay. He records writing letters to Justus, and this correspondence may well have been concerned with a desire on John's part to terminate their partnership. On September 21, Justus arrived with a man referred to only as Washington. Two days later the diary reads: "Melted the grease then went to Brooklyn to collect some money have sold out to Wash." The boy from Buffalo was ready to return home. Jus returned to Buffalo three days later, but John remained behind to wind up his business with Wash. He shipped the wagon to Buffalo on the 27th of September, and the next night took the boat for Albany. The trip was delayed six hours by fog on the river, but he arrived in Albany in time to catch the 1:15 for Buffalo, arriving at midnight on Friday the 29th of September. John D. Larkin's first business venture was ended.

After his return to Buffalo, John continued to work for Jus. Most days, and a good many evenings, were spent bringing in ashes, collecting and boiling fleshings, framing and cutting soap, or selling hard and soft soap uptown. He spent a good deal of time with his mother, where his younger brothers, William and James, still lived. In October he went hunting one day, while Jus kept an eye on the factory, and two days later it was Jus' turn to hunt. There was a singing school that met on Tuesday nights, which he enjoyed, and horseback riding (he paid 10 cents to rent the pony), and later when winter set in there was skating (which cost him 25 cents) and sleigh riding. He was clearly glad to be home in Buffalo with family and friends.

At this time an event occurred which made a considerable change in John's life. On November 20, 1865, his mother married Mr. Henry Hoag of East Hamburg. Although there is no mention of Mr. Hoag in the diary prior to this date, it seems safe to assume that Mary had known him for some time, and that the marriage was no surprise to her children. Mr. Hoag was a widower, who owned a forty acre farm in East Hamburg, NY. He was nineteen years older than Mary, with two grown daughters, Emma and Sarah. There is a fine photograph of Mary and the two girls dressed in the full-skirted fashion of the 1860's. (See page 103.) Emma and Sarah are seated and Mary stands between them, and, in spite of the stiffness required by photography at the time, it is a happy picture of three handsome women.

After his mother's marriage John continued working with Jus. He helped move Mary's furniture out to Hamburg, and there were frequent visits with the family out there. The two younger boys must have moved with their mother. John rarely mentions William, but there are several references to Alvin James' coming in to visit at the Weller's. Hannah, too, comes with "her sister, Mira," probably the sister of her husband, Hiram Jocelyn. Levi is not mentioned in the last months of 1865, and it seems probable that he was not in Buffalo.

With the close of the record for 1865, we come to a break in John D. Larkin's story. There are no diaries extant for 1866 or 1868. However, the diaries of 1867 and 1869 provide enough information to give a pretty clear picture of his development up to the time when he finally committed himself again, in 1869, to work with Justus Weller.

What stands out most clearly is the fact that John at the age of twenty was not ready to commit himself to business and the manufacture and sale of soap. We often note today that young people seem to lack direction, a sense of not knowing what they want to do with their lives. They try this and that, go back to school after false starts, and take no end of time before they settle down to their life's work. If we look at John's story, we find that this was as true in 1865 as it is today. However, there was a difference, and that difference was a lack of the pressure that plagues the youth of today. Reading John's diaries, one is struck by the fact that, while he worked fairly regularly and at various types of work, he often was "around home all day." When he was working for Jus, the hours were often irregular, and the work physically demanding and tedious, yet he seems to have had a good deal of freedom to choose his hours and work. The main point is that there is never a sense that anyone is putting any pressure on him to produce or to succeed. Always he is an important member of a loving, caring family, free to follow his bent and find his way. In these years, we see John vacillating between his love of the farm and the outdoors and a fascination with the world of business. His visits to the Durrant farm in Canada gave him fond memories of the rural life. On the other hand, the world of business offered the possibility of a prosperity that he had glimpsed in the milliner's emporium and at the Preston's, but never really known.

There is no record of John's activities during 1866, but the year 1867 found him living in Hamburg with his mother and stepfather. He began the year cutting wood on the farm, probably down in the swamp, as he refers to it in the 1869 diary. On January 21, John apparently came to some agreement to work for Jus and moved into his sister's home. He put in some long hours in the factory. January 23, he "worked from 7 to 2 o'clock in the night," and for several days thereafter he was in the factory all day tending to the boiling and crutching and framing of the soap. The weather was very stormy, it was bitter cold, and John soon found himself the victim of a sore throat. His condition worsened, he could take only a cupful of gruel, if he ate at all, and by February 3d Dr. Wiggins was called in. The good Doctor pronounced that John "was trying to have the quinsy." A popular remedy, syrup made from the "quinsy berry" (black currant), might have been perscribed, but if it was John makes no mention of it in his characteristically brief entries. The next day he was a little better, on the 5th he was still gaining, and on Wednesday, February 5th he writes, "Went out home today with father."

The rest of February and all of March, John was back and forth between his home in Hamburg and his home in Buffalo. In early February, he went to LeRoy to visit his sister Hannah, by then married to Mr. Taggart. He was in Hamburg in early March where he mentions attending "the debates at the corners," and a school exhibition one evening. He went to the Town meeting on March 5th and "had Dinner and Tea at Dave's." Dave appears to have been a close friend, but no surname is ever mentioned. He often gave John a ride to Buffalo when he took in a load of hay, or drove him back to Hamburg. John must have been doing some work for Jus, since he contracted with Mr. Bush for his "fleshings" on March 21. But he was back in Hamburg the next day and spent several days cutting wood for Mr. Ellis. At the end of March he "let Father have $41.00 to buy a cow."

On April 3, 1867, John took another important step in the direction of finding himself. He went out to Cold Springs and began work for his uncle Philo A. Balcom. The firm, P. A. Balcom & Son, having its office at the corner of Main and Ferry Streets, advertised in the City Directory as "manufacturers of / BRICK AND TILE / Red and White, (or light colored,) Pressed Stock, Sewer, Oven, Jamb and Hard Paving Brick, / Sewer Pipe and Drain Tile, all sizes constantly on hand. / CORNICE AND OTHER FANCY BRICK, MADE TO ORDER." The diary entry is brief as usual: "Have come to stay with Uncle at $25 per month." He was to work as a clerk in Philo's emporium, receiving room and board, until November, when he would take the next big step in his development.

The change to Balcom's was a beneficial one. He worked much more regular hours at the Balcoms' store and must have enjoyed the companion-ship of his cousin, Philo Jr., who was just three years his senior and with whom he remained on friendly terms until Philo's death in 1895. Sundays he went out to East Hamburg. The entry for Sunday, April 14th is typical: "Went out home afoot rode in with Dave in the afternoon. Church in the evening." There are frequent references to supplying money to Mother or Father toward "the cow." On July 5th there were fireworks down town, and on the 11th a festival in the Cold Springs Sunday School. On the 16th of

July, John went home to help with the haying, working all day the 17th and 18th, and taking a load of hay to Buffalo on the 19th. On the 20th, Willie brought him back to town "on a load of hay early." The entries for August consist almost entirely of the single word "Pleasant." Was this merely a meteorological observation, or a reflection of a general sense of well being?

In September Levi returned home from wherever he had been, and stayed in Hamburg. He came in to Cold Springs on several occasions while John continued to work there, and we can be sure he received a warm welcome and a place at Mary Balcom's ample table. On September 30, John notes "22 years old yesterday," and the next day, October 1st, the diary records some excitement over the opening of the State Fair. John shows interest in the attendance: October 2, 1867, "Had a little shower today 25,000 persons at the fair today," and, on the followng day, he writes: "A great many more to the fair today than yesterday. Mother and Willie were in today Willie went to the fair." The following day, a Friday, John went himself to the Fair (capitalized this time), but unfortunately gives no details, no reaction.

On several occasions in October John let his parents have money to pay for "the cow," and it becomes clear that he is investing seriously in the farm in Hamburg. On Sunday, November 3d, he "went out home with Levi," stayed all night and returned the next afternoon to Cold Springs, having acquired "a Produce Broker's License also bought ½ Doz. Crocks $4.30." The entry for November 9th reads "Levi came out. Finish working here tonight," signaling the end of his commitment to Uncle Philo Balcom. Sunday he stayed with Mary and Jus and went to church with Levi, and on Monday "came out home with Father." John spent the next three days cutting wood on the farm. One day he took 35lbs of butter to Buffalo which he sold at 35cents a pound. He made several visits to Le Roy, spent a whole day picking cider apples, made frequent trips to Buffalo for supplies, often walking home, and on Saturday, November 30, the diary reads, "Have taken the farm to work. . . ."

It is not at all clear from the sparse entries in John's diary what had motivated him to make this change. Perhaps there was something in his relationship with Jus Weller that kept him from making a firm commitment there. His step-father may have suffered from poor health; John records that "Father is sick again" in December. Also there may have been some tie-in with whatever Levi was doing. Could Levi have been occupied in some farming venture in Le Roy, perhaps with help from Hannah and her husband? John made frequent visits there as the change approached, and the brothers had been in unusually close contact during the month preceding the change. The entry for December 7, 1867, suggests this possibility, "Went to Buffalo Recd Butter Eggs & Fowls from Levi." Of course, we can never know the answer. All we can know is that at this point in his life, John D. Larkin made the decision to develop a farm, a decision that represents an interest in the land and its bounty that would remain with John throughout his life. I think we can be pretty sure, too, that this decision was made in an effort to support his mother and his younger brothers. Whatever the case, on December 26, 1867, John wrote in his diary, "Went up to the Corners. Paid Taxes." John had assumed responsibility for the farm in East Hamburg.

Again there is a break in the diaries, and we must pick up the narrative in January of 1869. This little book, which shows signs of hard wear, is inscribed on the first page "J. D. Larkin/ Buffalo/N.Y.", with the "Buffalo N.Y." crossed out and "Chicago Ill/ 822 Fulton Street" written below it. Glancing through it we see that John abandoned any regular entries after the middle of May, 1869, but that he carried it with him when he went to Chicago with Jus in 1870 and even when he returned to Buffalo in 1875 and set up his business at 198 Chicago Street.

The diary opens Friday, January 1, 1869, with a heavy snow storm from the NE and guests at the farm to celebrate the New Year. The big farmhouse was full with the Hoags and Larkins and Hannah's sister-in-law, Mira, and her husband, Gus, and the Phillips family (at least four). It was a happy time for them all gathered around the fire and in the warm kitchen where Mary and her step-daughters prepared the meals while the wind rocked the maples outside and the snow piled in drifts around the house and barn. As always John was busy with several projects to improve the operation of the farm. He was working on what he refers to in the diary entry as "the Power," a steam traction engine that he was preparing to use for cutting wood in the swamp. A man of short stature and average build, John loved the advantage over sheer muscle that machinery could give him. In addition to "the Power", he was making a "log boat" or sledge that he and James could use to haul the cut logs out of the swamp. But for all the work, there was time to have a bit of fun with the children and to enjoy his mother's cooking.

The next day dawned "lowry," and John took the machine down to the barn, finished the log boat, and went to town in the evening. Over the weekend it thawed, and Monday George Phillips brought the dreadful news of the sudden death of their little boy, Bertie. John carried the sad news to friends finding the roads very bad, and the funeral was held on Tuesday afternoon. The rest of the week was warm, and John worked in the swamp hauling logs. On Friday he was "working on Power took it down in the lot to set up." He worked all day Saturday on the machine. Sunday was "Pleasant/ at home." Monday the great moment arrived: he "started the machine this AM."

The rest of January and half of February were devoted to work on the farm, mostly running the machine, chopping, sawing and "skidding," as well as tending the farm animals, putting two loads of straw in the barn, and general "choring." John and James worked together, cutting mornings, hauling afternoons, or vice versa, usually working from morning until dark. However there is no sense of a slavish adherance to a schedule. Some days one or the other would take time off to go to town or to accompany Mary on some errand. The days alternated cold and blustery, warm and pleasant, and the work went on regardless of the weather. Hannah came to visit, and there were visits to and from Jus and Mary.

On February 18, John writes in his diary, "Pleasant. Picking up and Packing my things to go to Buffalo," and on the 20th, "Lowry. Thawing. Up town looking for situation."

There is no explanation of why John left the farm, and there is no looking back. He evidently did not find a situation, and on the 24th he is back in the factory working for Jus. However, this was not a permanent arrangement yet.

On the morning of the 9th of March, John left by train for Guelph and Winterbourne, Ontario, to visit his mother's family, the Durrants, there. After waiting six hours at the bridge, he reached Guelph at ten o'clock that night. The next morning his Uncle James Durrant picked him up and took him out to the farm. He was to stay in Canada for nearly a month, visiting around with various cousins and enjoying himself immensely. He attended the "social" in Winterbourne with James Durrant and his family the day he arrived, and then went home with Matt, with whom he seems to have stayed most of the time. There were several visits to Grandfather Durrant and to Uncle Donald and Aunt Sarah. Of the numerous cousins, he mentions Matt most often, but there were also Levi and William, John and Mary and Emma. The weather was generally cold and often stormy, but this never seemed to hinder the round of visitations. He participated in the farm work, threshing one day with cousin Matt, and on another day helping Matt take a load of wood down to Rosendale. One day Levi was "drawing stove bolts for J. F. [John Finly], but John "staid home choring in eve went to S. School meeting." Saturday, March 27, has a typical entry, "fog A.M. Pleasant P.M. we young folks went over to H. Wallace's to dinner/ Rebecca came down home with us." On March 30th "Matt was tapping maple trees today/ I was helping PM." On the 30th he writes, "Matt and I took Mary and Rebecca home I stay at Aunt Sarah's tonight." It took nearly a week to make the rounds and bid everyone goodbye, and, on Tuesday, April 6th, Levi took him down to Preston where he got the train for Niagara Falls and Buffalo.

The change had been good for John. Somehow this visit with his Durrant cousins had given him time to think through the question of what to do with his life, and he returned to Jus with a new determination to work for his brother-in-law. Jus was apparently building a new house, perhaps farther out Seneca Street, beyond the factory. John was occupied there, as well as at the factory, daily. One day he spent the morning learning how to ride "a velocipede." Brother Levi came on April 23d; on the 25th, he "went out to Mother with Jus & Levi;" and on Monday, April 26th, John writes "Jus Hired me at $25.+ Board." The die was cast, as he himself might have said, and John D. Larkin was henceforth committed to a career in business.

The diary entries continue for nearly a month, detailing John's preoccupation with the rough work of boiling, framing, pressing and cutting of soap, the collecting of tallow and ashes and the selling of the finished product, and, of course, the work on Jus and Mary's new house. Following the entry for May 23, 1869, the diary abruptly stops. The balance of its pages are filled with memoranda beginning with notes on glue making obtained from Jabesh Harris in November, 1869, lists of specifications for tools and machinery, price lists of labels and containers, and lists of freight charges from various cities, rental costs, records of various attempts to make one or another kind of soap, formulas for various mixtures of essential oils, and even an inventory of the "articles in Factory at 198 Chicago St. May 1st 1875." John carried this little book with him and used it to jot memoranda during the five years that he spent with Weller in Chicago, through his courtship and marriage to Hannah Frances Hubbard, the birth of his first child, his break with Weller and the eventful move to Buffalo.

Although John made no further record in the diary of his activities after May 23, 1869, there is evidence in a personal ledger that he kept from 1865 to 1875, that early in 1870 he went to Sandusky, Ohio, and set up there to sell soap for Weller in that city. Perhaps this was by way of scouting the territory for a move from Buffalo, part of the exploration that eventually led Jus to move his business to Chicago.

On the 1st of February, 1870, John was in Sandusky where he arranged to rent a shop from a Mrs. Boos at $2.50 a month. We can only speculate whether he lived and boarded with Mrs. Boos as well. Whatever arrangements he made for his own living, however, he went right to work purchasing 1,378 lbs of tallow @8¾ cents and shipping it off to Jus on that date. A few days later he paid $2.35 freight on 21 boxes of ML Soap, probably an all purpose household soap shipped to him from Buffalo, and a week later he received a shipment of both ML and Glycerin soap. On the 16th of February, John sold 600 bars of ML Soap and ½ gross of Glycerin Soap to H. & W. Ohley (retail merchants) who were to become regular customers in the next few months. The ledger entries suggest that he had labels and advertising slingers printed, and the record of work done on dies and a press may indicate that John also did some finishing work on the bars of soap before distributing them. The last entry in the ledger includes $5.00 for "Candle Moulds." Was J. Weller & Co. also in the business of making candles, as was true of many soap manufacturers, or were these merely for personal use? Nothing in the record gives an answer.

John must have wound up his business in Sandusky before the end of May and returned to Buffalo. He had scouted the territory for Jus and found it wanting. Though there was no formal partnership that we know of at this time (as there had been in Brooklyn in 1865), John and his brother-in-law worked closely together. We can assume that the decision to move the business to Chicago was made shortly after the Sandusky trial run, and that John had a strong voice in the decision. Before the summer was over, Jus sold his Buffalo business to the Harris Soap Company. He and Mary and the children packed up their belongings and prepared to leave their recently built house on Seneca Street. John paid a visit to the Hoags in East Hamburg, said good bye to his mother and brothers, and they boarded the train with high hopes for the adventure that lay ahead in the West.

---

[1] *Buffalo City Directory*, 1866. Advertisement.
[2] *BCD* 1853–1857.
[3] Surrogate Court of Erie County, File 13174.
[4] *BCD* 1857.
[5] Mildred B. Schlei, *The Larkin Company: A History*, Masters Thesis, University of Buffalo, 1932, p.5.
[6] *BCD* 1864. Mary Heath describes Weller in the 1870s as "a bearded man, with laughing brown eyes... He was full of pranks and fun..." *The Elbert Hubbard I Knew*, East Aurora, NY: The Roycrofters, 1929, p. 144.
[7] J. N. Larned, *A History of Buffalo, New York: The Progress of the Empire State Company*, 1911, p.66.

[8] Darwin D. Martin, to his brother William, copy in tissue letterbook p.208, Martin Collection, SUNY at Buffalo Archives.

[9] Preston's factory was located in Newark, but all of John's references to places and directions seem to indicate the Brooklyn area for their residence. Weller made arrangements for a location in Greenpoint which John could use as a base for operations when he started selling soap in the area.

[10] BECHS Archives, John D. Larkin Account Book 1865–1875 p.130.

[11] East Hamburg is now a part of Orchard Park, NY. The house, a section of which dates back to 1815, still stands at the corner of California Road and Route 20. I have been told that it was used at one time as a stage stop on the plank road between Lockport and Springville. It is clear from John Larkin's diary that his stepfather operated the property as a farm.

[12] Harry H. Larkin Jr., unpublished Larkin-Hubbard genealogy. John's older sister Hannah had married Hiram Jocelyn, probably around 1860. He died and she later married James S. Taggart of Le Roy, NY. by whom she had two children, Fred and Nettie.

[13] BECHS Archives, John D. Larkin Account Book 1865–1875, pp.40-53.

[14] It was the custom to indicate brands of soap with initials, and I have not been able to locate any trade names for Weller's soaps.

Chapter 3

Chicago 1870-1875

The years 1870–1875 were momentous ones in John D. Larkin's life. In those five years, he went to Chicago with Jus and Mary and became a partner in Weller's soap business; he met and married Frances Hubbard of Hudson, Illinois; and he made the decision to break with Weller and return to Buffalo to establish his own business. However, the record that has come down to us of this period is sparse. There is nothing to document exactly when the move to Chicago occurred or what prompted Weller to pull up stakes and make the trek west. The Buffalo City Directory lists his home and business address at 964 Seneca Street in 1869, and, as he is not listed in the Buffalo Directory for 1870, we can assume that he left the city sometime late in 1869 or early in 1870 for Chicago.

A business card indicates that Weller established his factory in Chicago at 913 South Halstead Street on the west side of the city under the name of "J. Weller & Co., Manufacturers of Staple and Fancy Soaps. . . Orders by Mail, or otherwise, promptly attended." This would have placed it in easy reach of the Union Stockyard and the supply of tallow and animal fats on which the business depended. He and Mary settled with their two girls, Hattie and Nellie, in a comfortable house on Sangamon Street on the West Side , and John moved in with them.[1] The house was not as near the factory as Jus would have liked, but it was in a good residential neighborhood, and he and John enjoyed the walk in good weather.

Chicago in 1870 was one of the fastest growing trade centers in the country. The burgeoning farms of the mid-west poured their produce into its vast markets—cattle, hogs, wheat and corn. The building trades were struggling to keep pace with the demands for construction, and a great variety of industries were competing for space and profit. David Lowe in the Introduction to his collection of eyewitness accounts of the Great Fire asserts that Chicago in 1871 was "the fastest growing city in the United States. It boasted more than 334,000 people and its 59,500 structures, spread over 23,000 acres, were valued at some $620 million. Its construction reflected a boomtown mentality. Speed was the name of the game."[2] Wood was used everywhere in the construction of homes, and even in the central business section the great buildings were of wood and iron with a veneer of stone or brick to establish an appearance of unassailable permanence. South and west of this commercial citadel lay the working class residential areas, consisting for the most part of wooden cottages, an area that was, as Lowe calls it, "a tinder-dry fuse waiting to be lit."

Weller's soap factory on Halstead Street was doing well when, on Sunday, October 8, 1871, at 9:00 o'clock in the evening, fire broke out in a small barn behind Patrick O'Leary's cottage at 137 DeKoven Street, only a few blocks away. Fanned by a dry wind from the southwest, the flames spread rapidly, jumped the Chicago river into the heart of the city, and by morning the proud city lay in ruins. Fortunately, Jus Weller's factory and home lay a few blocks to the west of the point of origin of the fire. As the conflagration spread to the east, the family would certainly have watched from their home on Sangamon Street with considerable anxiety, followed by relief when they realized that the wind was carrying the flames away from them. John and Jus almost certainly set out up Halstead Street, after checking on the Factory, to see what they could learn of the fate of the city.

Eyewitnesses later reported the frightening details of the spectacle that they would have witnessed: the deafening roar of the flames, the falling embers, the searing wind, the cries of the great crowds fleeing in panic from the city. Heavily laden wagons rushed through the streets heedless of the people on foot who were trying to drag or carry their valuables, women and children were knocked down, and the bridges were glutted with masses of humanity struggling to escape from the inferno. Another dimension of terror was added to the scene by the looters who took advantage of the chaos to seize anything of value that came to hand, only to be forced, in many cases, to abandon their loot and run for their lives when some building collapsed or exploded in their path. The fire lit the night sky until dawn broke over the smoking ruins and revealed the extent of the devastation to an incredulous population.

Whatever John Larkin may have witnessed of the Chicago Fire, it made a profound impression on him, perhaps awakening half forgotten memories of his father's heroism as a firefighter in Buffalo. In later years when John came to build his own factories and homes, he made sure that they were structures of brick and concrete and steel, invincibly fireproof.

It was in the spring of the year following the great fire that Jus Weller made a business trip to St. Louis. On the way he paid a visit to his uncle, Dr.Silas Hubbard, in Hudson, Illinois, a hundred miles southwest of Chicago, and set in motion the train of events that brought John Larkin and Frances Hubbard together. Frances' sister Mary gives a delightful account of Jus' unexpected appearance on a day in April when the family was busy in the yard with the annual chore of making soap:

> As we all sat or stood around the fire, the front gate opened, and a stranger came in, a bearded man, with laughing brown eyes, and with his tall silk hat pushed back too jauntily on his head to be the expected Baptist preacher. He walked right up to the kettle and taking the paddle out of my hands, said, "Here let me show you how to make soap." Father eyed him keenly, and when the stranger said, "I bet you don't know who I am," grasped his hand and said, "I do too, you are my sister Fanny's boy, 'Jet' Weller!"'. . . He told us that he had a soap factory in Chicago, and that he had married Mary Larkin of Buffalo, and that Mary's brother, John, was his partner in business. . . He divested himself of coat, collar, tie and silk hat, and donned overalls, and was soon deep in the business of making soap with us, declaring that he felt just like a boy.[3]

Jus arranged with his uncle and aunt to take his cousin Daisy Hubbard with him, and, when he returned, to take Frances (or Frank as she was called) home to Chicago for a visit. He was as good as his word, and a few days later, Frank boarded the train for Chicago with her new found cousin. There is no record of that two week visit in the summer of 1872, but Mary's account of her own visit to the Weller's later that summer can give us some idea of the reception that Frank received:

> And now the jolly cousin [Justus Weller], tall hat as ever on the back of his head, was at the train to meet us, driving a black horse in a top buggy, and we drove to his home on the West Side in Sangamon Street. The sound of the horses' hoofs on block pavements, the smell of hot sprinkled streets,

the high church spires, dark dripping tunnels, the balconies and pretty flower boxes everywhere, and ruins upon ruins, for this was the year after the great fire, all made a lasting impression on the child's memory. Cousin Mary and her children gave us a cordial welcome on their balcony, and their home seemed very elegant with its Brussels carpets, its dining room in the basement, and its running water. As we stood on the balcony, a small, handsome, dark-eyed young man, with brown side whiskers, and a very firm, white chin, came running lightly up the steps. Mother greeted him as "John" and told him how she had held him in her arms when he was a baby. . . John started to speak to me, but I was bashful and dodged back through the French doors, he following me around and around until it became a game, and finally reversing, he caught me and kissed me.[4]

Frank wrote home glowing accounts of her wonderful visit, of the sights and excitement of the great city. There was shopping to be done, there were fine theatres to attend and spacious parks where one could stroll at leisure. Church on Sunday must have seemed an elegant affair after the simplicity of the little church in Hudson. Above all, there is every reason to believe that Frank was strongly attracted to the handsome young man with the whiskers who was her cousin's business partner.

The exact chronology of John's visits to Hudson is difficult to determine. Mary Heath suggests that his visits came soon after Frank's stay in Chicago. However, the ledger that John kept of his expenses makes no mention of a trip to Hudson until June 20, 1873, and all subsequent visits were meticulously entered. Whatever the case, Mary records that the visits to Chicago were returned:

...and it is my impression that John came many times—for I can remember him attending church sociables, playing on the melodeon, singing hymns, at picnics, and nutting parties and many outdoor frolics, and skating gracefully and dexterously on our ponds to the delight of the villagers, but best I remember him sitting with Frank under the sweet-briar rose bush, engaged in long and earnest conversations.[5]

These are clearly the fond memories Mary cherished of her childhood, and they are valuable for the insight they give into John's character. His love of picnics and "outdoor frolics," his fondness for music—"playing on the melodeon"[6], his joy and skill in skating, and underlying all, his profound thoughtfulness. It is interesting, too, to note that on July 11 John bought a copy of the *Phrenological Journal*, a publication dear to his future father-in-law's heart.

Frank kept the letters that John wrote to her during their courtship, neatly folded as received and tied with a pink string, some hand delivered when they were together, most of them mailed to Hudson from Chicago. The letters leave no doubt about John's complete surrender to the charms of Jus Weller's pretty cousin and his firm determination to marry her if she will have him.

The letters begin October 25, 1873, with an invitation written on J. Weller & Co. stationery extended by Jus and Mary for Frank and Daisy or Mary to come to Chicago "and make them a real good visit." The letter is signed "From J. & M.J.W. per Cousin John." John points out that the "Great Exposition" will close the following Friday, "so that you will have to Hurry up here in order to see the Wonders of the Nineteenth Century."[7] The ledger suggests that the girls made it to Chicago for the Exposition. Indeed that the closing had been postponed, for John recorded expenses relating to the Exposition from November 1st to the 13th including car fares and ten cents for a shave on the 1st and the 13th.[8]

The next note has no envelope, and clearly was hand delivered to Frank who was already the Weller's guest:

Chicago, Nov. 5 1873

Miss Audacious Stunner Having heard you make a remark, Equivalent to saying that you would like to Attend Prayer Meeting some evening while in the City. I take this liberty of requesting your Company to the "Young Peoples Meeting" on Monday Evening Nov 10th, believing that you would enjoy yourself there in a manner that you could not elsewhere
 Most Respectfully
 Your Obedient Servant
 Adolphus GreenPickle[9]

That playful invitation was written on Wednesday. On Thursday, we learn from a later letter, that John made Frank an offer of marriage:

What passed between us Thursday Evening was on my part intended as a "Bona Fide" offer of marriage, and I thought you would so understand it—though you apparently made light of it—perhaps my manner was too "Matter of Fact" or too "Business like" and unromantic to become such an Occasion, but nevertheless I was Sincere. I have no wild Protestations of Love to make—nor Boyish Dreams about the future to offer—but am prepared to give you more Practical and substantial Evidence of the motives which actuate me in doing thus, motives which I have thought by your actions, (since you came to Chicago) were reciprocated by you. I will rest the case here—trusting that you will give it your carefull and impartial consideration before making your decision, and that you will speak your mind Freely and Candidly in your reply to this

Yours Truly
John[10]

This is only the first of a series of letters in which John pleads his case. On November 11, he writes again asking Frank to reconsider his proposal. He acknowledges his awkwardness and "unfeeling manner" and understands that she might find it difficult to believe in his sincerity, but feels that she would forgive and understand "could you see behind these Stolid and indifferent Exterior Appearances, that are the results of commencing life's Battles in early Boyhood and the struggles through which I have passed."

John refers to his visit to Hudson the previous summer, the acknowledged purpose of which was to become better acquinted with Frank, "and in the Happy Hours we passed together there, I found that there was a oneness of Feeling and Thought that I had never experienced before with anyone."[11]

Before she left Chicago, Frank apparently went so far as to say that she felt they "could live Happy together" and John replies, "is it not a duty we owe to our Creator and ourselves to be happy, and to seek Happiness in all Honorable and Legitimate ways. . ."[12] With characteristic good sense and restraint, he continues to urge Frank to wait on any final decision until her return home.

By the end of November, Frank was back in Hudson and had told her mother of the engagement. Through the winter months many letters passed back and forth between Hudson and Chicago. Having won his suit, John's letters take on a playful intimacy. Frank sent the picture he requested, and

John tells her how he could only steal a glimpse of her when he received it at the factory:

> . . . *as we were very busy Framing Toilet Soap, + therefore had to attend right to Biz; but didn't I make up for that, 'down in our Talking Room' after all the rest had gone to bed last night—shall I tell you how? perhaps you won't object, so I'll venture. Well—I tipped my chair back, + put my feet on another one, then set you on my knee, (now don't look cross about it) and let you talk to me through your letter.*[13]

Beneath John's sense of fun, however, there lies always the simple sincerity, the unwavering good sense and quiet devotion to whatever course he chose to take in life. In contrast, Frank had the volatile temperament of the true romantic. She suffered frequent attacks of "the Blues" that often led to doubts about herself and the impending marriage. John wrote at length and with unshakable patience to allay her fears and to assert his firm belief in the steadfastness of their love. Through February and March the letters reflect Frank's ups and downs, but at the end of March she chose Sunday, May 10, as the date for the wedding. John's letter in reply is characteristic. He tells how after supper Jus handed him some bills and the mail that had come to the factory that day. Jus and Bert and Mary were watching him closely, and as soon as possible he retired to his own room:

> . . . *to learn the contents of the envelope that had caused such a flutter. . . Frank, I feel just as though I want to say something but cannot express my feelings at all. I believe there are times in this life when 'Silence is more Eloquent than speech' such with me is now . May Our Heavenly Father Bless + Guide us both.*[14]

During the next month John found himself under considerable pressure. As early as February, Justus had been considering plans to enlarge their business, and in early March he determined to move the factory from Halstead Street to a "large Brick Soap Factory cor Hoyne + Hubbard Sts northwest of Union Park."[15] At the same time Jus and Mary decided to move their home to a location within sight of the factory at 763 Fulton Street. For some time, John had been dissatisfied with the arrangement of boarding with the Wellers. His relationship with Mary had soured for some reason, and he expressed the hope to Frank that she would not be too intimate with

Mary. At the same time, John wrote, "as for my Business arrangements—I think very likely Justus and I will continue together for several years yet."[16] With the expansion of the business, he and Frank would be able to afford a home, and the prospective bridegroom lost no time in hunting for a suitable place for them to set up housekeeping. During all of April, John's every waking minute was taken up either with the demands of the old factory, the move to the new factory at 141 N. Hoyne Street, or the few hours he could afford for house hunting. He and Jus worked long hours, often staying at the factory until late at night.

John's letter of April 19, 1874, is worth quoting in full for the picture it gives of the situation and the man:

> *Chicago Apr 19/[18]74*
> *Dear Frank*
>
> *Yours dated 14th was received Thursday. We have been very busy this last Week—it seems to take us a long time to get things to running all right, but I hope we will get a stock of Soap ahead in the next two weeks, though just now it looks rather dubious we are so far behind our Orders. There is so much more to look after up here than there was at 913 S. Halstead St, that I don't find any chance to go down Town, or any where in the day time, + consequently don't know what I'm going to do about some things here but will find out shortly. My trip to Hudson will necessarily be a short one, so your suggestion in regard to the Eleven Oclock train is agreeable to me, though I'm afraid you will find it a very tedious journey. As yet I can't say what day I will meet you at "Normal Depot" but think Friday or Saturday, May 8th or 9th, which would you prefer? I presume I shall have to start from the Factory with carpet bag in hand + run to catch the Train + with my working suit on, not having time to change. I guess you begin to think that I am not __proud__ + care very little for appearances, well I'll have plead guilty, + offer as an excuse __ignorance__, really I sometimes think I ought to have a Gaurdian [sic] (Angel or some other kind) to look after me + tell me what is right + what should be done. Frank I sometimes feel as if I have been very presumptious in some things, in the last few months + that you will be sadly disappointed upon a more intimate acquaintance, but I find*

some consolation in the thought that "True Love" is willing to overlook much.

Well! in regard to the "it" that is to "happen in the Parlor" on the 10th Proximo; D.V. I want to say let it be done as quietly + with as little preparation + ado as possible. I think you will understand the spirit in which I say + mean this, for you know I'm Bashful + Awkward, and don't know how to act when I get in Company. I haven't any Friends that I think care enough for me to accept an invitation to be present + therefore concluded that I wouldn't invite anyone. A little bird has just come in at my window attracted by the gaslight—it is storming so I didn't go to church this evening, I caught the bird + carried it downstairs + put [it] in the cage with one of the canaries. I commenced writing this letter this afternoon but have been interrupted by one and then another. Levi is here for a few days + of course we have had to visit some. Jus and Mary have been telling him some things, Real + Fancied in regard to you and I, for the purpose (I suspect) of drawing me out, but I laugh when they laugh, + as hearty too—+ help them to joke John—+ enjoy the fun with them. + then occasionally say something to make them think they are humbugging themselves. but I must close for I have another to write to a Cousin in Buffalo who wrote and asked me for certain information over a month ago. I guess she thinks I'm rather dilatory in answering. With kind regards to all, not forgetting yourself + hoping to hear from you again soon I remain Yours Truly
J.D.L. [17]

On May 3d, John wrote that he would "leave Chicago on the 9:30 train via the Chicago & Alton R. R., arriving Normal about 2:30 PM next Friday, May 8th." Frank, perhaps teasing a little, has asked in a letter if he knows what he is doing in getting married, and his reply, more than half serious, is characteristic:

I think I do; but I haven't attempted to forecast the future, or anticipate the results or consequences of this step. . . preferring to await developments. Then, too! I think partici-

pation is much better than anticipation & therefore await the latter . . .[18]

He closes with a request that she write "Tuesday in time for the mail" that he might hear once more from Frances Hubbard.

Only a few days before he was to leave for Hudson, John found a home for them—a flat in the upper part of a two story cottage at 822 Fulton Street, a block west of Jus and Mary's home.[19] In an addendum to the same letter, John looks forward to meeting Frank in Normal on Friday. Mary Heath recalled that the groom arrived on Saturday. Perhaps the fifty five years that intervened played tricks on the memory of the woman who was a girl of ten at the time. In any case, we can assume that the Chicago and Alton R.R. bore the bridegroom safely to Normal where he was doubtless met and driven to Hudson in the Doctor's buggy.

It was the custom among God-fearing folk for the bride to remain in seclusion before her wedding, and Mary tells in her account how "the bride remained concealed, and retreated upstairs at the sight of an approaching caller, never leaving the house during her last week at home," for to do so would have branded her as "a shameless girl."[20] Mary also notes that the younger sisters were baffled by the fact that the prospective bride was often in tears. They, of course, knew nothing of the emotional turmoil that Frank had experienced in reaching the decision to marry John, to leave home and to commit herself to life in an unfamiliar world with a relative stranger.

The wedding day dawned bright and mild, and the fruit trees in the yard were heavy with bloom. Because the marriage was a religious ceremony, the strict Sabbath rules could be relaxed. The guests, who could expect a celebration not usual on so solemn a day, assembled in the parlor at five o'clock. The minister, followed by the bride and groom, came down the front stairs. They took their places, with Bert, the best man, and Rose Chadbuourne, the bridesmaid, before the sofa. John was handsome in his best broadcloth suit, and Frances in "stiff pearl gray silk poplin, real lace at her wrists and neck, and the groom's gift of pretty pendant coral ear-rings and brooch" was radiant. The ceremony was simple and brief, followed by "a solemn charge and a long prayer."[21] There were maternal tears and hearty congratulations and a great spread of home made rolls and cold meat and coffee and cake—and more cake! Mary and Daisy and Honor had seldom seen such abundance and frivolity, and certainly not on Sunday. The party was soon over, however, when the church bells rang for evening service, "and we all, including the bride and groom, walk across the road to service."[22] That same night John and Frank boarded the midnight train for Chicago, and their life together began.

The newlyweds must have been relieved to have the uncertainties of courtship over and the distance that had separated them closed. At last they could talk without having to seek a precarious privacy and they could share the consummation of their love and the joy of building a home together. John, of course, was no less busy at the factory, and Frank must have missed him during the long working hours. Of course, she, too, was busy settling the flat, buying the necessaries to set up housekeeping. And she was not without company, for John's letters and Mary's book both indicate that Mother Hubbard and the sisters were urged to visit in Chicago and did so. The Larkins and the Wellers both loved the theatre, and Mary tells, in her account of those visits, of Mother Hubbard's being taken (with considerable reluctance) to see Joseph Jefferson in his famous interpretation of Rip Van Winkle—"and she was so carried away and fairly intoxicated by it that when she came home she rehearsed it till we too could see Rip and the goblins."[23]

The spring passed swiftly into summer, and in July Frank went back to Hudson while John made a trip to Lockport, NY, to close up the branch of the business that Weller had maintained there. John was gone from July 23d to August 5th, and his letters, addressed to Mrs. J. D. Larkin/ Hudson/Mclean Co/Ill, tell how much he misses his "Dear Wife." He visited the family in Buffalo, staying with his mother in East Hamburg and with Auntie Balcom in the City, before he returned. His letters written on the train travelling the Michigan Central from Chicago to Buffalo and then back to Chicago on the L.S. & M.S. R.R. are filled with detailed observations of the trips from Chicago to Windsor, Ontario, Hamilton, and Buffalo, and then from Buffalo to Chicago, through Cleveland. The two weeks were long and lonesome without his bride, and, when he did get back to Chicago, he found that Tom and Jennie Preston had arrived, and Jus had gone to Hudson with them and left the factory in John's charge. It was a blow that he couldn't go straight to Hudson and join his wife. He wrote frequently to Frank, often several letters a day, and finally she returned to Chicago with Jus and Tom and Jennie.

There is a break in the letters between August 6, 1874 and February 9, 1875, and in that time the association with Justus Weller reached the breaking point. John had felt unsure of Jus' judgment, and in August, when Jus was in Hudson, he had asked Frank to observe Jus carefully and keep her ears open to learn what she could of his position. By February John had reached the decision to go into business for himself. On February 8th, he wrote to Frank in Hudson that he and Jus had discovered that they were losing money. Somehow Jus had not kept track of accounts as he should have, and, although he promised to do better in the future, John's confidence was shaken beyond repair.[24] The decision to leave Jus was undoubtedly influenced, too, by the fact that as the year came to a close Frank was well into her first pregnancy. Soon they would be not just a couple, but a family, and John was acutely aware of the responsibility that the future held. On the 18th or 19th of February, John was again reunited with Frank in Hudson. He was able to report that he and Jus had discussed the break-up of the partnership, and Jus agreed that it would be fine for John to go east as long as the territory could be divided to their mutual satisfaction.

On March 4, 1875, Charles Hubbard Larkin was born in Hudson, and on March 13, John and Justus signed the articles of dissolution of J. Weller & Co.. John sold his interest in the company to Jus for $9,579.06—$8,345.57 to be in cash and the balance in soap in the hands of agents in New York and all soaps ready to be shipped to them. Shortly thereafter John left for the East to scout out a place to establish his own business. Bert Hubbard was in Ithaca, travelling in the area for Weller at the time, and they hoped to meet in Albany. John apparently went first to Boston, where he found "not very much dif— in cost of stock, bones etc.between this point + Chicago." However, rents were higher in Boston, and he had not been able to locate a factory that he would move into. All in all Boston did not much appeal to him. Perhaps in Albany "I—we can do better." He also planned to spend a night in Syracuse, to visit family in Buffalo, and perhaps "to stop at Cleveland for an hour or so."[25]

With hindsight, of course, we know the outcome of this trip. After a characteristically thorough investigation, John decided on Buffalo as the ideal location for his business. On April 9, 1875, he signed a lease agreement with E.B. Holmes for a factory at 196–198 Chicago Street in Buffalo "for the sole manufacture of soap." Rent for the 3,000-square foot plant was $500 a year. He made the trip back to Chicago and settled final arrangements with Jus. Bert Hubbard had been working as a salesman for J. Weller & Co., and one of the decisions that had to be made was whether he would continue with Weller or go to Buffalo with John and Frank. His loyalty to his older sister and his admiration for his brother-in-law made that decision easy. Years later he wrote of John:

I came to Buffalo with a man eleven years my senior. He
was born in Buffalo of English parents, had learned to make
soap, keep books and do business. He was an active, ener-
getic, simple, unpretentious honest man, with a firm hold on

the Scottish virtues of industry, economy and truthfulness—
he did not have much money, but he knew what he wanted
to do and he did it.[26]

John found time to be in Hudson with his wife and little Charlie before he returned to Buffalo. It must have been a time of great happiness for both of them with the future secured at last. All that remained was for John and Frank to make the move from Hudson to Buffalo and establish themselves and their family there.

Family tradition, supported by Mary Heath's account[27], has always held that John went back to Buffalo and was followed at a later date by Frank and Charlie accompanied by Bert. However, a postcard written by Bert and recently found among John's papers raises a doubt about this version of the move to Buffalo. Postmarked from Albany, N.Y. April 18, and headed "Sunday afternoon," the card is addressed to John at his Chicago address, 822 Fulton Street, and reads:

John—Your letter of 15th rec'd this morning. I expect to arrive in Buffalo Friday morning at 6:20 will find a good boarding place for us all & have the landlady wait dinner so when I meet you at 1:10 we can all sit down & enjoy a good square meal, excepting Charley who I suppose prefers following out Dame Nature's plan & has not yet acquired that visciated taste for "boarding house hash"—EGH

The 18th of April, 1875, was a Sunday, and Bert's message certainly suggests that John and his wife and son were to arrive in Buffalo on Friday, April 23.[28]

In any event, John lost no time in setting up in business after May 1st and in finding suitable lodging for his family in a pleasant residential neighborhood at 213 Eagle Street. His diary contains, as previously mentioned, an inventory of the equipment and materials already in the factory on Chicago Street. He set about hiring a small crew to work with him in the manufacturing of soap, with the idea that, as soon as they could begin to build a stock, Bert would go on the road to sell. On the first anniversary of their marriage, May 10, 1875, John and Frances were together in the city that was to be their home for the rest of their lives.

---

[1] Mary Hubbard Heath, *The Elbert Hubbard I Knew*, p. 146.

[2] David Lowe, *The Great Chicago Fire*, New York: Dover Publications, Inc., 1979, p.1.

[3] Heath, p.144.

[4] Heath, pp.146-147.

[5] Heath p.147-148.

[6] BECHS Archives, John D. Larkin Account Book, 1865–1875, p. 108. On October 17, 1873, John paid 83 cents freight on a melodeon shipped from Buffalo.

[7] JDL to FH, 10/25/1873.

[8] BECHS Archives, JDL Account Book 1865–1875, p. 109.

[9] JDL to FH, 11/5/1873.

[10] JDL to FH, 11/8/1873.

[11] JDL to FH, 11/11/1873.

[12] JDL to FH, undated letter, hand delivered.

[13] JDL to FH, 12/9/1873.

[14] JDL to FH, 3/31/1874.

[15] JDL to FH, 3/4/1874.

[16] JDL to FH, 4/12/1874.

[17] JDL to FH, 4/19/1874.

[18] JDL to FH, 5/3/1874.

[19] JDL to FH, Monday Eve 10 P.M. [May 4, 1874]

[20] Heath p.155.

[21] Heath p. 156.

[22] Heath p. 157.

[23] JDL to FH, 5/4/1874 and Heath p. 157.

[24] JDL to FHL, 2/8/1875.

[25] JDL to FHL, 3/24/1875.

[26] Heath, p. 159.

[27] Heath p. 158.

[28] Mary Heath quotes her brother as writing "I first arrived in Buffalo on May tenth, Eighteen Hundred Seventy-five." (p. 158). Plans may have changed after Bert wrote the card, or the passage of years may have dimmed the focus of hindsight.

Chapter 4

Success and Sorrow 1875-1885

The Buffalo that John and Frances Larkin came to in May of 1875 was a rapidly growing city with a population well over 150,000, a thriving inland port and manufacturing center. By 1880, the Buffalo Business Men's Association noted proudly on its stationery a population of 250,000; 162 miles of paved streets; 248 passenger trains daily, as well as "638 miles trackage in city limits;" an estimated 2,500 manufacturies; an unlimited water supply; "50 miles of street railways;" receipts for 5 million tons of coal, 395 million feet of lumber, 95 million bushels of grain; live-stock sales of 2 million dollars; grain elevators with a capacity of 14 million bushels; natural gas, now in use; and "Health: the very best."[1] No wonder that John chose to settle here. Buffalo was the right place to be for anyone who wanted to launch a business.

With his small crew (Mike and Jimmie are mentioned in the diary), John set about getting the "works" at 196 & 198 Chicago Street in operation. The property leased from Mr. Holmes consisted of a two story brick building 25 by 60 feet and a frame barn. The brick building, containing 3,000 square feet of space, had previously been used for the manufacture of soap and contained some of the necessary equipment. The inventory in John's diary lists a number of items, among them 19 frames and frame bottoms on wheels, 1 press (legs broken), 1 lot soap racks, 1 crutcher, 1 iron kettle, 6 buckets (good for nothing), some rope and tackle.[2] All this had to be put in order and the necessary additional equipment (at least one large kettle, several small kettles, dies, boxes for packaging and shipping, etc.) had to be purchased to get the business started. Sources of tallow and other raw materials were readily available locally, and John lost no time ordering what he needed. By mid May they were ready to begin manufacturing soap, and on May 18 John purchased one barrel of tallow from M. Rothschild of 162 Exchange Street at $23.01 a barrel. Larger orders followed within a few days, and John was able to find additional sources. Sweet Home Soap, a yellow laundry soap, was the first product. The new company, J. D. Larkin, Manufacturer of Plain and Fancy Soaps, was launched.

Bert may well have been out on the road in these early days selling the soap already in the area that Weller turned over to John by the terms of the sale agreement. John funded his new venture with $6,000 of the capital that he brought with him from the sale of his share of the business to Jus. This would need to be augmented promptly from the sale of soap, for the process of setting up the factory and turning out the first product would be costly. In addition to the cost of supplies and equipment, rent for the factory was $41.66 a month, and there were the wages to pay (Bert received $60.00, Mike $20.00, and Jimmie $10.00 in July).

While John was occupied with the factory, Frank was busy settling their new home at 213 Eagle Street and caring for little Charlie. There is no record of what the couple brought with them from Chicago, but a list of expenses for domestic items in John's diary is interesting both for what it includes and for the prices listed: "Carpet border, $14.00; Stand, $6.00; Chairs + repairs $12.00; Wash stand,$4.00; What not, 4.50; Globe + dishes, $3.50; Can (oil), $.35; Bed Stead, $4.50; Mattress, $4.50; Springs, $5.00; Commode, $5.00; Baby Carriage $16.00; Looking Glasses, $3.00; Stove, $2.50; Crib Cradle, $9.00; Bedroom Carpet, $11.00; Bible, $16.00. [Total], $120.35."[3]

Bert stayed with John and Frank from time to time when he was not on the road, but most of the time Frank and John and little Charlie would have found themselves at home in their own world. They quickly made a place for themselves in the community, attending church on Sundays and renewing old acquaintances of John's. They would have visited Auntie Balcom and Uncle Philo in their ample home at Main and Ferry Streets and proudly introduced them to their infant son. There would have been visits to the farm in East Hamburg where John found his mother holding things together, but not without considerable pain. Mary Hoag's world had seen some sad changes in the five years that John was in Chicago. She must have been distressed by the breakup of her daughter Mary's marriage to Justus Weller. After the divorce, Jus moved his operations to Detroit, leaving Mary and the two girls on their own in Chicago. Closer to home, both her daughter Hannah, who had married James S. Taggart of LeRoy, and her son James, who lived at home in East Hamburg, had died in 1874, aged 34 and 26 respectively. William, her youngest surviving child, lived with her. Badly crippled, he was unable to work, and Mary cared for him until his death in 1904.[4] John felt a very close bond with his mother and his siblings, looking out for their welfare and supporting them in every way that he was able. His mother must have welcomed John's return to Buffalo and the prospect of a growing family of grandchildren to bring fresh interests into her life.

The summer and fall of 1875 passed quickly with all the excitement of a new life. Before they knew it, Christmas came—little Charlie's first—and Christmas was always a very special event in their lives. There was a tree, probably a small one that first year, and decorations and presents. Then, in February or March, Frank told her adoring husband that there would soon be an addition to the family. John undoubtedly received the news with his usual calm, but Frank knew from the light in his eyes and the smile he gave her that he was very happy. Little Frances Elberta would be born September 9, 1876.

John's business was thriving as well. Brother Bert and his crew of salesmen covered an ever wider market. John had taken on several more hands at the works, and spent long hours there himself to keep the supply flowing to the salesmen. The years with Jus, the experiments with the making of soap, and the long hours spent tending the boiling kettles had paid off. John was an expert at mixing the fats and the lye and bringing the smelly brew to just the right consistency. He had developed sound formulas for the special perfumes that the toilet soaps required, and shortly after they began production the little plant was turning out toilet soap—Creme Oatmeal—as well as the more mundane laundry soap.

Sometime in 1875, the ubiquitous Elbert Hubbard, ever on the lookout for good men to join his sales force, discovered several men whose association with the company was to have lasting significance. In Philadelphia he made the acquaintance of the Coss brothers, William Henry and Daniel John, and in Columbus, Ohio, Bert found Frank Martin, whose brother Darwin would play a large role in the history of the company.[5]

The Coss brothers of Philadelphia first appear among the salesmen in the record kept during 1877–1878 of the soap shipped out to men on the road. Darwin Martin's account of their coming to Buffalo indicates that in 1879 "the brothers Coss were given work with an advertising-wagon, posting bills, etc. They lacked self-confidence and therefore never braved merchants other than harness-makers, to whom they could sell Larkin Jet harness soap. But when they were separated from their advertising wagon they 'streaked it' to Buffalo on their own volition, coming in, August

1880."[6] In 1881, William is listed in the City Directory as "foreman w[ith] Larkin & Co, b[oarding] Southern Hotel." Daniel is listed as "clerk, b. Southern Hotel." They had clearly settled in Buffalo.

William Coss, the younger and more able brother, may have had some experience in the making of soap. Martin writing in 1909 at the time of their retirement speaks of him as a chemist.[7] However, he states that, "Mr. Larkin taught William the art of soap making, to his own great relief from the onerous duties of the kettleroom."[8] In all probability, what he knew of chemistry he learned on the job. By 1881 John had given William the position of superintendent of the factory. Daniel Coss, for whatever reason always remained somewhat in the shadow of his brother. The two were inseparable, sharing a hotel room as long as they lived in Buffalo, and apparently having little or no social life. They were quiet men, honest and industrious, and John, with his usual keen insight into character, must have realized at once that he could work with and rely on the Coss brothers. Dan started as a night-watchman and eventually was placed in charge of the shipping office. They became stockholders when the business was incorporated in 1892, and served as Directors of the company until their retirement in 1909.

As mentioned before, Bert Hubbard was out on the road most of the period from 1875 to 1878, when he entered into a partnership with his brother-in-law. With his growing army of salesmen, he spread the news about Larkin soaps from Boston to Chicago and from Milwaukee to New Orleans. At first the method of selling, which the salesmen referred to as "soap slinging"[9] was a simple matter of going door to door and offering a box of soap for the lady of the house to try. A few days later the "slinger" would return and collect payment for whatever the lady cared to buy. This was much the same approach that John had used in 1865 when he was selling in Brooklyn for Jus Weller.

As the reputation of Larkin soaps spread and the volume of soap required to satisfy the demands of Bert Hubbard and his slingers grew, John saw within the first year that the little factory on Chicago Street was hopelessly inadequate.

In 1877, John purchased two 30 ft. lots on Seneca Street at the corner of Heacock (now Larkin) Street, each 150 ft deep.

On these lots, at 663, 665 and 667 Seneca Street, were built the first of the factories that would eventually spread over many acres. The new factory was a frame building, fifty feet wide and eighty-four feet long. "Its equipment consisted of a six horse power steam engine that rocked the building, two soapkettles and two hand presses."[10] By 1880 when the Coss brothers arrived in Buffalo, the volume of business had increased enormously, and in that year the company entered a three-year period of tremendous growth. "The factory ran three years night and day. . . and the firm was out upon such a solid foundation that old building B was built in 1885 at a cost of $12,000 as a result."[11]

Meanwhile, with the prospect of a growing family, John and Frank became increasingly interested in owning their own home, and, with the growing success of the business, there was no reason not to look about for a house of their own. Frank took an active interest in the search, and, in late March or early April of 1876, she found exactly what she wanted at 218 Swan Street. The property was owned by Francis H. Root and his wife Delia. On April 18, the deed and bond in the name of Frances H. Larkin were signed. An interesting sidelight on the relation between the sexes at the time appears on the Bond in the form of a deposition by a Notary Public to the effect that "the said Francis [sic] H. Larkin on a private examination by me apart from her husband acknowledged that she had executed the same freely + without fear of her husband." The Bond also contains a record of payments of interest and principal up to April 1, 1885. They would live in the brick house at No. 218 Swan Street for the next eight years, and four of their seven children would be born there.

Not long after they had moved into No. 218 Swan, Frank, perhaps at her brother's urging, set out on a journey to Philadelphia, where the great Centennial Exhibition had just opened. In a letter dated June 9, 1876, John wrote to Frank at 320 Front Street, Philadelphia, Bert's address during the Exhibition. From the letter, it would appear that Frank and Bert travelled east, going to Albany, then down the Hudson to New York and on to Philadelphia. She was six months pregnant at the time, but undaunted she took little Charlie with her.

What a lark the trip must have been for the ebulliant brother and his adoring sister! She would have been carried on his enthusiasm through all the rigors of travel, and she may have welcomed a change from John's serious absorption in the manufacture of soap. Given Frank's intellectual curiosity and love of history and art, the Centennial would have drawn her like a magnate. The fact that the Emperor of Brazil had shared the honors with President Grant at the grand opening on May 10, 1876, would have added a dimension of romance that Frank would have loved. She must have been impressed by the industrial wonders exhibited in the great Machinery Hall, but the exhibits of exotic and domestic plants in the vast glass house of the Horticultural Hall would have been more to her taste. Frank would have been particularly attracted to the Art Gallery with its display of

European and American sculpture and painting (a central attraction of which was the "Marriage of the Prince of Wales," loaned by Queen Victoria), and the United States Building with its rich historical exhibits would have fascinated her.[12]

In his letter, John hints that he, too, may pay a visit to Bert during the summer, if business takes him east. We can safely assume that it did. Even more than Frank, John would have been fascinated by Machinery Hall whose exhibits were driven by the giant central Corliss Engine. There he would have found "the Power," as he had called the steam traction engine of his logging days in East Hamburg, magnified almost beyond belief, for here was one giant steam engine supplying mechanical energy to hundreds of exhibits. The Corliss engine "rose forty feet above its platform; its cylinders were of forty-four feet diameter and ten feet stroke, and the flywheel, weighing fifty-six tons, was thirty feet in diameter."[13] This monster powered such exhibits as the corset weaving machines, the Lyall positive-motion loom, the pin machine which struck 180,000 pins per day, automatic spool-cotton winding machines, watch-making machines, carpet looms, a model tobacco factory, India-rubber shoe machines, printing presses, a Jacquard loom, and automatic machines for making envelopes and paper collars.[14]

These marvels of industrial power would have had a strong appeal for the young man who had struggled with boiling and crutching soap in his brother-in-law's factory and with the hard physical labor of running a farm.

John's letter to Frank goes on to tell that he had been "out to the springs" and found the family there [the Balcoms] "all about as usual. It does seem a little lonesome here without you and Charlie. . . Had a letter from Bro Thomas yesterday. I will enclose it herewith with the hope that it will not shorten your visit in Phila." Whether the prospect of Brother Thomas' visit caused Frank to hurry home, we cannot know. However, in the family Bible (perhaps the one that John purchased a year earlier for $16.00) there is a certificate of Holy Matrimony signed by Evan J. Thomas, Minister of God, who had performed the marriage ceremony two years before in the little house in Hudson, Illinois. The date of signing is given under "Buffalo, N. Y., June 14th 1876." Frank later made a note at the bottom of the page, "Made out when Mr. Thomas visited us on his way to Europe in 1876." He must have been one of the first visitors to the new house on Swan Street. The summer following Brother Thomas' visit passed quickly for the young couple, and on September 9, 1876, a baby girl was born at 218 Swan Street. Frank agreed to name her Frances, as John wished, as long as she could add Elberta in honor of her brother, and, to avoid confusion, little Frances soon came to be known as Daisy.

The remaining years of the 1870s were busy and eventful ones both at 663 Seneca Street and at 218 Swan Street. With twenty five men on the road covering an ever widening territory, the demands on the little factory were staggering. John had to hire on more help to handle the process of manufacturing and to train men in all the demanding jobs he knew so well from the days with Weller: the management of the soap kettles, the crutching, the pouring, the cutting and the stamping. A few girls were brought in to handle the wrapping and packaging of the finished product. Careful records had to be kept in the big ledger books of what soaps were shipped to which salesmen, and a close accounting kept of each man's sales. John, with his training at Bryant and Stratton Business School, kept all the records himself in the first years, working at a stand-up desk with patient attention to detail. Supplies had to be ordered from the box manufacturers and printers, and this became a major concern as the number of different soaps increased. The large scrapbook of promotional material shows examples of labels and box covers for as many as nine different soap products in the year 1878. These range from "Boraxine" soap powder through a variety of laundry soaps to "Jet" harness soap, "Oatmeal" toilet soap and Glycerine. Small wonder that by 1878 John realized that he needed his brother-in-law closer to home and more involved in the mechanics of production and promotion.

The two men entered into a partnership in that year under the name of J. D. Larkin & Co., with the apparent understanding that Bert would handle the advertising and John the manufacturing of the product and management of the accounts. The firm claimed a capital of $18,000 (JDL $12,000 and EGH $6,000) and profits and losses were to be shared (JDL $\frac{2}{3}$ and EGH $\frac{1}{3}$). This partnership was the first of several entered into prior to the incorporation of the business in 1892. In 1885, the partnership was re-drawn with a capital of $77,000 (JDL $47,000/EGH $30,000) and a 50/50 division of profits. Apparently John's hopes of anchoring Bert in Buffalo had not been entirely realized. The new partnership of 1885 specified that Hubbard "agrees to devote his entire time to said business."

At the same time the new agreement specifically states "that in consideration of the extra amount of capital furnished by the said John D. Larkin he is to have the privilege of devoting as much of his time and attention to the business as he chooses and he can withdraw his time, tact, skill and knowledge from the business and devote them to any other business without prejudice to his interest in the firm of J. D. Larkin & Co."[15]

This proviso was an important one. Deeply involved in the soap business as he was, John was not entirely sure that there were not other areas of business that might be more lucrative, and he was always on the lookout for other possibilities. John was living in a time when the potential for progress seemed unlimited. Electricity was making its appearance and opening new vistas of power and progress. The telegraph and the telephone were only the beginning in the procession of inventions that would transform the world, and John was interested in them all. With a friend and distant relation of Frank's, Edward Cole, John became interested in an inventor working in Brooklyn to develope a printing telegraph. He and Cole supported A. C. Robbins with loans and personal encouragement, making trips to Brooklyn to confer and observe the inventor's progress. Robbins, for all his inventive genius, was apparently incapable of organizing his work or keeping orderly accounts, and his health was frequently in jeobardy as a result of overwork. Characteristically John exhorts him in letters to try to organize his work, to be systematic and to guard his health. There are also letters that indicate that the two men were interested in the development of a folding machine that would facilitate the making of packaging materials. This would have been of particular concern to John for he and Bert were increasingly in need of boxes and wrappers for the various lines of soap that they were introducing to the market.

In 1878 and 1879, the growing factory at 663 Seneca Street was often working around the clock to supply Bert and his crew. Many a man would have buckled under the strain of work and the increasing load of responsibility at home, but not John D. Larkin. His steady, unflappable temperament, his long experience with hard work—the soap slinging days in Brooklyn, the gruelling labor of the farm in East Hamburg, and the long hours tending Jus Weller's soap kettles and accounts in Buffalo and in Chicago—all gave him ample preparation for the long hours demanded by the "works" at 663 Seneca Street. Unlike his older brother, Levi, John had developed early in life an unusual tolerance for the tedious drudgeries of day to day existence. He accepted these as the natural components of any progress towards success, and he expected to spend 10 to 12 hours a day at his business.

On the credit side of the ledger, John had every reason to feel successful. Everything that he had been building toward was being realized at 218 Swan Street. His beloved Frank was a wonder at managing the establishment, seeing to the modest domestic help they were able to afford, shopping and planning for the house, paying the interest on the mortgage and the city and county taxes with the money that he provided and devoting herself to the loving care of the children. In the summer of 1877, Frank was pregnant again and it was arranged that her sister Mary, then just thirteen, would come to Buffalo "to go to school for a year."[16] Frank must have welcomed the companionship of her little sister and the help she could give with the children. John Jr. was born on October 28, 1877, and John valued every minute that he could spare from the "works" to be with his family. The Larkins had a fine horse and carriage, and there were picnics in Delaware Park—"The Park"—on fine days. They held pews at several of the local Baptist churches—Cedar Street Baptist and Prospect Avenue Baptist—and attendance at services on Sunday was a high point of the week. In addition there were church socials, charity concerts and festivals, art exhibitions and theatres to attend. The family particularly enjoyed the theatre, and Buffalo's Academy of Music and several other theatres offered frequent opportunities to see the great stars of the day in everything from Gilbert and Sullivan to Shakespeare. In 1878, Madame Helena Modjeska brought her famous Shakespearean troup to the Academy, and in May John records $2.50 in his personal account for "Modjeska (tickets)."[17] Some years later, John and Bert would give the great lady's name to their most popular line of soaps and cosmetics. Another aspect of the growing cultural life of Buffalo was the burgeoning Library, and John and Frank and Bert all took an active interest in its growth. John paid $1.50 for his "Library ticket" on August 19, 1878.[18] All of these social and cultural points of contact offered the opportunity to expand and cement the circle of acquaintances that John was already making through his business contacts. The Larkins were active participants in the growing community where both had their roots.

It was in 1878 that a thirteen-year-old boy became an employee of John D. Larkin & Co. under the aegis of his brother Frank Martin. Frank was slinging soap in the eastern territory and was anxious to provide for his young brother, Darwin, who was miserable in the home of his battling father and step-mother in Nebraska. Arrangements were made for Dar to travel to Newark in August, and there he was initiated into the mysteries of "soap slinging." In his unpublished diary, D. D. Martin gives a colorful and often detailed account of those days:

> *In our work, Frank and the older boys walked all day. A fifty-cent box of oatmeal soap (twelve cakes) weighed three pounds. We carried two boxes every time we left the wagon.*

*At picking-up time each half-day I was in the wagon driving
the horse and receiving from the other members of the crew,
three, including Frank, the picked up boxes and recondition-
ing them for reslinging in the latter part of each half-day.*[19]

After Frank Martin and his crew had pretty well covered Newark and
the Oranges, they were ordered to take their remaining supply of soap and
move their operation to Boston. During their stint in Boston, John D.Larkin
visited the city on business and, of course, checked up on the local sales
force. Darwin remembers him in his autobiography as "a quiet spoken
young man, with a black full-beard, in his thirties."[20] The sight of young
Darwin working the wagon for the slingers must have stirred memories of
his own days as a young boy working to help support his mother and his
siblings. John always had a soft spot in his heart for a boy who was energetic
and willing to work. When he found out that Darwin was making only three
dollars a week, he promptly raised the lad's salary to five dollars.

The following summer, Bert informed Frank Martin that his work in
New England was finished, but that he would be given work as a traveling
salesman in the middle west. The firm was moving away from the old
technique of slinging soap and concentrating more on custom sales to
general stores and other merchants who would buy the products in large
quantities. Indeed, by 1880, the company was handling its wholesale
accounts under a separate name—The People's Mfg. Co.. Sales to individuals were still handled under the name of J. D. Larkin & Co., but these were
handled more and more by mail, and the days of "soap slinging" were
virtually over.

On the morning of August 7, 1879, John arrived at the office to find
Frank Martin and Darwin waiting for him. Frank, who was heading west,
was anxious to settle his little brother in some employment, and he approached John about the possibility of Darwin's working in some capacity
for J. D. Larkin & Co. in Buffalo. Dar was a small boy for his age, and it
was clear that the heavy work in the factory among the older and bigger
boys and men would not be best for him. After conferring with Frank Martin
and talking a little with Darwin, John realized that here was the very fellow
he needed to help him with the by now overwhelming task of keeping the
books. He would need to be trained, but John could see no problem there.
The boy was obviously smart and accustomed to work. To test him out, John
assigned him the task of indexing a tissue copy-book in which were kept
copies of letters written in pen and ink. John had meticulously kept business
letters by this pre-carbon technique, but there had never been time to

properly index the record. The boy found two boxes used for shipping the soap, nailed them together to make a seat that would bring him to the level of the stand-up accountant's desk and set to work. As Dar himself tells it, "So, one hour after my arrival in Buffalo...I became the first and at that time the only hired office-worker of J. D. Larkin & Co.; until then all office-work was done by Mr. Larkin himself at a stand-up bookkeeper's desk."[21]

John must have sent word to his wife by his driver that the Martins were there and that he had hired the boy, and Frank, knowing that the occasion called for a celebration, decided that a picnic in Delaware Park would be suitable. She sent word to John that she would pick them up at 663 Seneca street with the horse and buggy in the afternoon, and they would all drive out to The Park together. Frank and the girl who helped with the children and the house "prepared a bountiful and delicious picnic-luncheon."[22]

With little Charlie in the buggy, she drove to 663 Seneca to pick up her guests, only to find that John was delayed by an essential oil salesman with whom he must conclude business. Little Charlie elected to remain at the office with his father, preferring public transportation to the buggy. With Frank Martin at the reins, Mrs. Larkin and Darwin set off for the Park "where Mr. Larkin and little Charlie, by horse-car, soon joined us."[23] On that festive note began an association that would endure for over forty five years.

The association was not without its ups and downs in the early days. In his *Autobiography*, Darwin recounts several episodes that might well have led to his dismissal. They are worth looking at for the light they shed on the character of his employers. Martin's work required him to have access to the business ledger books, order books and tissue letter-books. These were always locked in the office safe at night. The young lad was prompt at work and impatient to begin, but he had to wait "for the arrival of the horse-and-buggy which always marked the beginning of Mr. L.'s business day." The bright boy soon learned the numbers of the combination as he watched John open the safe, and, impatient to get to work, eventually decided to open the safe himself. "Mr. Larkin said nothing, but the next morning I found the combination had been changed." Weeks went by. Martin, chafing at the loss of valuable time, soon had the combination again. His impatience eventually got the better of him, and he determined to open the safe and get to work. "Nothing was said but the combination was not changed again and I opened the safe daily."[24]

By 1881, Martin proudly informed his sister, Delta, that he held the unique position of being the only boy employed by any firm in Buffalo as

59

Head Bookkeeper. In April of that year, he made a serious error in judgment. Copying letters for the firm, he made a second tissue-copy of a business letter from Hubbard to John's brother Levi and sent it on to his brother Frank Martin, who was then selling soap for J.Weller & Co.. Bert discovered what had happened, conferred with John, and they concluded to discharge the boy.

> *I was sure to be in the office in the evening, and so they had returned to it to give the boy a talking-to and send him on his way. They had raised my pay to six dollars a week that very morning, and my mis-step was a poor return for their generosity.*
>
> *My employers gave me a "third degree" that evening. I wept for my sin and think I begged so hard for another chance that it was granted and we never had occasion to revive the subject. Perhaps my frequent references in my letters to the nobleness of my employers had laid the groundwork for their concession to me.*[25]

As mentioned above, Bert and John realized by the summer of 1879 that the old method of "slinging" soap was no longer best for the rapidly expanding business with its country-wide reputation. Through the People's Manufacturing Company, they would sell to merchants in large quantities and under custom labels. At the same time, of course, the mail order sales to individuals would be expanded through advertising in local papers throughout the country, as well as by soliciting names of reliable prospects from current customers. The decade of the 1880s was to be a period of enormous growth for the Company. Numerous enticements were introduced to attract customers. One of the first of these was the inclusion of chromo cards with the soap. "The People's Pets" were large 8- by 9½-inch cards offered with Boraxine and Sweet Home Soap in 1880. These proved very popular, and the next few years saw a flood of titles and pictures, often in series, included with Boraxine and other soap orders, and even offered individually "to anyone on receipt of two 3 cent stamps."

The story of the advertising that built the Larkin enterprise from a modest soap manufactory in 1880 to a nationally known mail order house by 1900 deserves a study of its own. It can be found in the large scrapbook preserved in the library of the Buffalo and Erie County Historical Society. Here are samples of slingers, letters, newspaper advertisements, chromo cards, order forms, box wrappers—all of the colorful paraphernalia of the ad-man of the period. Between them John and Bert conducted an intensive campaign to sell the Larkin products by appealing to the interest of the solid working and middle class families in godliness, cleanliness and self-improvement. Through friends of John and Bert, the Edwin Alden Company, a newspaper advertising agency in Cincinnati, they placed ads in newspapers and magazines throughout the country. In addition to the ads, they contacted publishers asking them to present testimonials in their publications so that they would not appear to be paid advertisements, and they requested lists of "the best citizens of your city." Lists of heads of families and respectable citizens were also solicited from current customers. In grateful return for these favors a case of Sweet Home Soap or some other product would be promptly sent. By 1887 all salesman had been eliminated, and J. D. Larkin & Co. depended entirely on advertising and mailings to promote its business.[27]

Probably Hubbard's greatest advertising gimmick, the Great Combination Box, first launched in October of 1885, was an incredible bargain. It consisted of 100 cakes of Sweet Home Family Soap and an assortment of toilet soaps together with six boxes of Boraxine (an ideal cleansing agent consisting of pure soap and borax pulverized together)—enough to keep an average family clean for a year. In addition to the soaps, each box contained an assortment of perfume, cold cream, sachet powder, tooth powder and a Napoleon shaving stick. The next year, John and Bert put their enthusiasm for Christmas to profitable use by offering the "Mammoth Christmas Box" which, in addition to the soaps, perfumes and other products, contained "gifts"—"Playthings, etc. for the Babies and sundry useful and amusing things for the older folks," as well as silver plated spoons, glove buttoners and hair pins, thread, handkerchiefs (gentlemen's and ladies'), biscuit and cake cutters, assorted pictures suitable for framing, two celluloid collar buttons, engravings, art studies, scrap albums and even a tack hammer. All this went for six dollars on thirty days approval, freight paid (points east of the Mississippi only). J. D. Larkin & Co. could make it Christmas all year round.

To further attract new customers, our entrepeneurs offered prospective customers who would "send cash for a Christmas Box and agree to recommend the Soap to three or more friends" a set of 15 volumes of the works of Charles Dickens or the Waverly novels of Sir Walter Scott, 25 in all, sent free of express or delivery charges. Much of the advertising was aimed at church and Sunday school groups through various Christian publications. What better way to attract people of substance and integrity who could be relied upon to deal fairly with so generous an offer?

Clearly all these tactics worked. An 1890 advertisement proudly states that 91,000 boxes were sold in 1889—$546,000 from the Mammoth Box alone. J.D.Larkin & Co. was riding a wave of success that would carry it through the great depression of 1893 and into the twentieth century.

While the 1880s brought the first great wave of prosperity to John's business, they dealt less kindly on the home front. The first years of the decade were happy enough. Frank was enjoying her new baby, Edith May, who had been born on May 7, 1879. Charlie and John were healthy, growing boys on whom she doted, and between them in age was Frances Elberta whom she called Daisy after her sister. Daisy, a beautiful girl, with her mother's black hair and big brown eyes was old enough to help with the new baby. Frank was too busy tending to the children's needs and the social duties of a young wife to be concerned that John spent long hours at "the works," and that his business and social contacts took much of his time. In 1881 another baby came; little Harry Hubbard Larkin joined the clan. John was essentially a family man, and, however much of his time was absorbed in managing the business in those early days, Frank could always count on his being home at dinner time, bringing little presents for the children, joining in their games, planning excursions into the country and picnics in the park. For all his devotion to duty and serious attention to the demands of work, John was a man who realized fully the value of recreation and physical exercise. He loved the outdoors, was an accomplished skater, enjoyed games with his boys and made a habit of taking daily exercise. Sometime in the 1880s he joined the YMCA, where he attended classes in the gymnasium, much to the delight of his young clerk who recorded the fact in his diary.[28]

As the family grew and their social horizons broadened, the Larkins began to feel the need of a larger house in a less commercial neighborhood. With the rapid growth of the business, John was in a position financially to move, even to build a house for himself. He and Frank looked at the property that Mr. Charles J. Hodge and his wife were offering for sale on Hodge Avenue and they liked what they saw. It was a new neighborhood, near enough Delaware Avenue to give convenient access to downtown in one direction and Delaware Park in the other. The lots were ample, Elmwood Avenue had convenient shops nearby, and Jehle's fine grocery store, just around the corner at Elmwood and Bryant, even boasted a telephone. John made arrangements to obtain a mortgage loan from Messrs. Taylor and Crate, and on February 23, 1884, a warranty deed was issued conveying the property at 125 Hodge Avenue from Mr. Hodge and his wife to Frances H.

Larkin. Undoubtedly the couple lost no time in getting plans and starting the building of the house at that address. They arranged to rent a house at 230 Bryant Street while their house was being built and moved their family from 218 Swan Street sometime in the spring. This was a time for family moves: Bert and Bertha moved to East Aurora in April.

In 1882 a group of prominent Buffalo men joined together to form the Idlewood Association. Such familiar Buffalo names as Daniels, Stafford, Nelson, Riegel, Dann and Foster were among the signers of the original Certificate of Incorporation, and the membership list for 1888, headed by J. N. Adam, reads like a Who's Who of business and professional Buffalo. John had become acquainted with and respected by these men as he moved up in the business world, and they welcomed him as a charter member when he paid his dues of $100 in September of 1882. The group acquired a very desirable tract of land on the south shore of Lake Erie and the east bank of Eighteen Mile Creek where the creek flows into the lake. The area was easily accessible from Buffalo for the B.N.Y.& P. Railroad made regular stops at North Evans nearby, and it was only a carriage drive of several miles to Idlewood. Here members camped during the summer months on lots purchased from the Association and planned eventually to build more permanent summer homes for their families. In the spring of 1883, John purchased Lot Number 8 at a cost of $100, and Frank and the children were delighted at the prospect of summers in the country. The next two summers passed quickly for the family. They lived in tents, set up on wooden platforms, undoubtedly had cooking arrangements for each family and a maid to help with domestic chores and to look after the children. For Charlie, Frances, Johnnie and Edith, the summers must have seemed like one long picnic. They played on the beach, swam in the lake, and had boats for rowing and fishing. Harry, just beginning to walk, loved the sand and the water and just being with the older children on the beach, always under nurse Annie's watchful eye.[29]

Papa, as the children always referred to John, had to be in Buffalo at the works during the week, but he boarded the train every Saturday punctually at 5:30, was met by Frank with the carriage at North Evans and was playing with the children in less than an hour. On numerous occasions, John invited his young clerk, Darwin Martin, to spend the weekend with the family, and from the accounts Darwin has left in his diaries we get a glimpse of life at Idlewood.

Saturday, August 2nd [1884], *Took the train B.N.Y.& P.*
with Mr. Larkin at 5:50 and arrived at Idlewood about an
hour later. Mrs. Larkin met us with the carriage at the depot.
At bedtime Mr. Larkin and I went in bathing: it was delight-
ful. Spent my first night in a tent.
On a second visit the bathers included Mrs. Larkin and
quite a party. Sunday, I took a long walk alone on the beach
in the morning. Idlewood is a delightful place, a splendid
way to live. With Mr. Larkin and two of the children took a
boat-ride, I did the rowing. Rained all night.[30]

Darwin recalls one episode that tells something of John's integrity:

I think I must have deliberately omitted, as unpleasant, the
episode I remember which cost the Larkin children their
water spaniel. He took a nip at one of James D. Stafford's
small boys. Theirs and the Larkin's tent were near, Mr.
Stafford demanded the death of the spaniel before sundown
lest hydrophobia. Mr. Larkin was a man of peace and I led
the spaniel to a neighbor outside the grounds where he was
dispatched with a shotgun. Oh, oh! A rifle would have done
a far neater job! I asked Mr. L. if I might 'lose' the dog. He
rejected my plan.[31]

The young clerk who would later commission one of Frank Lloyd
Wright's finest Prairie houses, was greatly impressed with life at Idlewood
and wished he "had the money to place my family in well-to-do circumstances and thus make them as happy as Idlewood people."[32]

The joys of Idlewood were to be short lived for John and Frank. The
following summer a tragic accident occurred that ended the visits to Idlewood forever. On Sunday, August 16, 1885, six-year-old Edith May and
John Jr., not quite eight years old, were playing on the beach, reportedly
without supervision. Perhaps Annie was watching two-and-a-half year old
Harry elsewhere. The children tired of skipping stones and hunting for shells
along the beach and decided fire would be fun. Accounts differ as to the
nature of the fire. The *Commercial Advertiser* reported that the children
"built little ovens with stones and built fires in them."[33] Other accounts,
including Darwin Martin's diary, refer to a bonfire. Whatever the nature of
the fire, little Edith somehow got too close, and her frilly Victorian clothing

caught fire. Terrified she started to run to the camp for help, but Johnnie and another boy, realizing the need for immediate action, intercepted her flight and got her down to the water's edge where they sat her down and splashed water over her head and body. Despite their quick response, Edith was severely burned. She was carried to the camp by her frantic parents and given whatever treatment was known at the time. There were no burn treatment centers then, no mercy flights. John must have managed to call Bert Monday at the office. (Telephones were still scarce, but J.D. Larkin & Co. had had a private phone since 1881.)

Bert lost no time getting to the stricken family at Idlewood. He arranged for young Martin to go to East Aurora to look out for the place there, as Bertha was away, and caught the afternoon train to North Evans. On Wednesday Bert must have brought Darwin the sad news that Edith died at six o'clock that morning. Bert returned to Idlewood, and Darwin went back to East Aurora with instructions to drive the carriage to Buffalo in the morning to meet the funeral cortege at the depot. Darwin's diary entry for August 20, 1885 records the sad occasion:

> *Arose at five o'clock, ate breakfast, and per Mr. Hubbard's instructions drove to Buffalo, left E. Aurora at 5:25 arrived in B. at 8:50 just in time to get to depot and meet the funeral, drove from thence to Forest Lawn in the procession, witnessed the ceremonies in the Chapel vault where Edith's remains repose for the present. Worked in afternoon. Returned to Aurora by rail in evening. Very tired.*[34]

On the 23d of September, 1885, John purchased a lot in Forest Lawn for the sum of $552.50. It must have been one of the saddest purchases he ever made. Edith was the first member of the family to be buried there. John continued as a member of the Idlewood Association, carrying out his duties on the board until he sold his lot in 1892. Frank never went back.

---

[1] Blank sheet of Buffalo Business Men's Association stationery in author's collection.

[2] JDL, Diary 1869. This list occurs under the date November 25, 1869 followed by note: "List of articles in factory at 198 Chicago St. May 1, 1875."

[3] JDL Diary 1869, Cash Accounts, undated.

[4] The exact nature of William Larkin's affliction is not known. Harry H.

Larkin Jr. reported to me that he was in a logging accident on the farm in East Hamburg. A letter dated as late as 1960 from Mary Weller's daughter Nellie suggests another explanation: "Uncle Willie had that Locomotor Ataxia as you thought & also had both ankles broken trying to walk one time." (letter to Ruth Larkin Robb from Nellie Joachim, Lincoln Nebrasaka, March 4, 1960)

5 Darwin D. Martin, *Autobiography*, SUNY Buffalo Archives, p. 70.

6 Ibid.

7 *Ourselves* Vol.5, No. 21, July 1 1909, p.1.

8 Ibid.

9 Horton H. Heath, "Elbert Hubbard—Salesman," *Printer's Ink*, October, 1931, p. 54.

10 Ibid.

11 D.D. Martin letter to JDL Jr. SUNY Buffalo Archives and author's collection.

12 *Souvenir of the Centennial Exhibition*, Hartford, Conn.: George D. Curtis, 1877. pp. 26-27.

13 Ibid. p. 26.

14 Ibid.

15 BECHS Archives, Larkin Company Inc. Records.

16 Mary Hubbard Heath, *The Elbert Hubbard I Knew*, p. 161.

17 BECHS Archives, Larkin Company Inc. Records, JDL "Personal Account 1878" (loose sheets in Bound Vol.#3)

18 Ibid.

19 D. D. Martin, *Autobiography*, p.44.

20 D. D. Martin, *Autobiography*, p. 45.

21 Ibid. p. 53.

22 Ibid.

23 Ibid.

24 Ibid. p.55.

25 Ibid. p.79.

26 An excellent beginning has been made by Craig R. Olson in an unpublished thesis *The Evolution of the Larkin Company and Its Advertising Premiums, 1875–1900*, SUNY College at Oneonta, 1993.

27 Schlei, p. 11.

28 D. D. Martin, *Diary*, March 3, 1884.

29 BECHS Archives, John D. Larkin Letterpress Copy Book p. 172. hereinafter referred to as JDL LCB.

30 D. D. Martin, *Autobiography*, p. 89.

31 Ibid.

[32] Ibid.

[33] *Commercial Advertiser*, Buffalo, Monday, August 17, 1885, p.3. The accident was also reported in *The Buffalo Daily Times* and the *Buffalo Daily Courier*, August 18, 1885.

[34] D.D. Martin *Diary*. August 20, 1885.

Chapter 5

Healing and Building

As indicated in the previous chapter, the decade of the 1880s was marked by important changes in the direction of J. D. Larkin & Co., and John must have found the press of business almost a relief in the wake of Edith's death. In the spring or early summer of 1885, there was a crying need for more space and equipment in the factory in order to meet the demands of Bert and his salesmen for soap and other products. John determined to tear down the frame structure at the rear of the brick building that fronted on Seneca Street and erect a larger building. The three story frame building was razed and a new five story addition built in its place. Darwin Martin tells in his diary of the trouble they had with pilfering during the demolition:

> *The neighbors around the factory carry away the lumber as the carpenters tear the old building down and take everything they can find movable* [sic]. *Have to watch them closely, jumped from an office window after some Irishman and sprained my thumb.*[1]

With the change in sales methods already noted—the shift from soap slinging to mail order—came the first use of the slogan that was to become the hallmark of the Larkin business: Factory to Family. The first Modjeska toilet soap was brought out in 1886, to be followed by Modjeska perfume, tooth powder and sachet. The chromo cards continued to grow in popularity, and more substantial premiums were offered in the form of solid silver pieces from Gorham. Soon the Company was able to claim a factory capacity of 10 million pounds of soap per year. As previously noted, the company sold 91,000 of the "Sweet Home" Combination Boxes in 1889. Hubbard, the ad man, was bursting with creative ideas and writing copy that often foreshadows his later work. Favorites with customers who were hungry for culture were the series of biographical sketches of famous statesmen and authors that look forward to the "Little Journeys" published later by the Roycroft.[2]

In 1890, Hubbard's huckster's zeal got the better of his judgment. At a time when John was away from the office on business, Bert ran a series of ads in newspapers and church publications offering "Six Solid Silver Spoons GIVEN GRATIS to each reader. . . who orders a Mammoth 'Sweet Home' Box, and agrees to recommend 'Sweet Home' Soap. . .to three or more friends."[3] The only problem was that the spoons were of German silver, a cheap substitute for the real thing. Orders poured in, but, as Martin put it, "soon the publicity degenerated into notoriety,"[4] and angry customers were demanding satisfaction. When John returned to Buffalo, he was appalled at the situation. This was not the kind of business dealing that he wanted his name to be associated with. He insisted that every set be replaced with a set of sterling silver spoons. There is no record of the confrontation that must have taken place between John and Bert, but it may well be that John's faith in his brother-in-law suffered a fatal blow. Regaining the confidence and good will of customers required strong measures. Martin records that the episode considerably diminished sales, but that the new approach of offering service rewards to customers for getting other customers "smothered us under an avalanche invoked by the law of geometrical progression."[5]

Perhaps as a part of the effort to overcome the effects of the silver spoon debacle, the old $6.00, freight paid offer was changed to a box consisting of the same 100 bars of "Sweet Home" soap, "but with an itemized *priced* list of Boraxine and toilet soaps of a total of nearly $11, the whole offered with a Prem[ium], oil brass floor lamp,—'Chautauqua Piano Lamp'—for $10."[6] This innovation ushered in the immensely popular line of Chautauqua Premiums, of which the best known is the Chautauqua desk, today a popular item among collectors.

First introduced in 1892, in an ad in *The Ladies' Home Journal.* The Chautauqua Desk/Combination Box offer became the force that drove the explosive growth of the company between 1892 and 1900. The Combination Box offer was soon dropped and the premiums offered with any ten dollar order of products, or individually from the premium lists issued from 1893 on. In 1894, sales of the Chautauqua Desk alone amounted to $15,425.

By 1899, the peak year for sales of the Chautauqua Desk, the figure had grown to $80,635. On one day alone in February of 1900, 2,036 desks were sold.[7] The desk remained in the Larkin Catalog until 1920, and accounted for an average annual gross profit over those years of $87,378.

The desks were initially supplied to the company by two different manufacturers: Spencer, Barnes & Stuart in Benton Harbor, Michigan, and the Minneapolis Office and School Furniture Company in Minneapolis. Martin in his *Autobiography* has an amusing account of the first order sent to Spencer, Barnes & Stuart:

> *Mr. Hubbard found at D. E. Morgan & Sons, a furniture store, then in the building occupied in the nineteen thirties by Oppenheim, Collins Company, the desk, at about ten dollars. He sent it to S. B. & S., or somehow acquainted them with its specifications and asked for a quotation. Mr. Barnes quoted four dollars. Mr. Hubbard asked him to make a sample. The sample was delayed. That was because Spencer had such contempt for Barnes' flirtation with a soap factory for a combined writing desk and bookcase in oak. He had made the sample of ash. When it was ready to ship Barnes discovered the mistake, Spencer made his protest, "Oh, those soap men won't know the difference between oak and ash." Spencer made it over again and Barnes shipped it by express.*
>
> *Mr. Hubbard was well enough pleased and sufficiently in earnest to write a pen-written postal card ordering five hundred desks. Messr. Spencer and Barnes were delighted with the order, But Spencer was made to eat humble pie; so much so that for a long time after he made himself scarce. When Barnes' tall figure climbed the stairs of their two story factory, Spencer would manage to to be going downstairs at the other end of the factory when Barnes head emerged from the stairs at the other end, because he knew that Barnes had that postal card in his pocket always ready to show him again.*
>
> *The second order was for two thousand, and from first to last I suppose S. B. & S. made several hundred thousand desks.[8]*

It was undoubtedly the success of the Chautauqua Desk and other

Chautauqua Premiums that carried the Larkin Soap Mfg. Co. through the serious depression of 1893 and on to its unparalleled success at the time of the Pan American Exposition in 1901.

The decade of the Nineties was filled with a great many changes and anxieties for John D. Larkin, both at the office and at home. With the introduction of the Chautauqua line of premiums, Martin's "avalanche" had begun, but the initial rush was to be slowed temporarily by the panic of 1893. In 1892, Bert announced his decision to leave the business, go to Harvard and become a writer, a move that undoubtedly delighted Frank as much as it must have puzzled John. The same year J. D. Larkin & Co. was reorganized and incorporated as The Larkin Soap Manufacturing Company. At home John and Frank were involved with a growing family. After the loss of a son, Hubbard, who died in infancy in 1887, the couple must have welcomed the arrival of Ruth Read Larkin, born August 14, 1891. Charlie and John Jr. were 18 and 16 respectively in 1893, and John was anxious to provide for their education. In addition to the immediate family, there were many problems with brother Levi and sister Mary during these years, and John's mother, living in North Evans and caring for William, was in precarious health. Altogether the 1890s were a period of mixed joy and anxiety for the Larkins.

On January 6, 1893, Elbert Hubbard resigned from the business to pursue his ambitions as a writer and his passion for Alice Moore. Bert had arranged to sell his 13,000 shares of Larkin Soap Mfg. Company stock to John in return for stock of the Hyde Park Land Syndicate, Ltd., the Delaware Parkside Co. (real estate companies) and three promissory notes payable in January and July of 1893 and January of 1894 respectively. The original agreement was signed by John and Bert November 1, 1892.[9] Neither could have anticipated then the problems that would arise before the settlement of this arrangement five years later.

The great panic of 1893 made itself felt in the spring, and its effect was devastating to the Larkin Soap Mfg. Co. whose widespread business depended heavily on western states. Darwin Martin records for that year:

May 31st. L. S. M. Co. getting awfully hard up. The western states are hard hit by the panic which hits farmers first. . .August 22. For many weeks, perhaps three months, the Larkin Soap Manufacturing Co. could pay no salaries at all to the Coss brothers, Miss Anna Bellis ($15 per week) or *myself. . . November 11th. Mr. Larkin declines any increase for next year.*[10]

In this situation, John was unable to meet Bert's notes without drawing on the resources of the company. This he flatly refused to do. Bert insisted, and filed a law suit in July, 1893, in an effort to force John's hand. The correspondence between them grew bitter, but John remained immoveable. He would not jeopardize the business. Eventually a settlement was arrived at out of court. Bert wanted securities and notes that he could convert into cash at the bank. John assigned his life insurance policy over to Bert, was able to arrange to make payments at such time as business improved, and was often forced to borrow money to meet payments.

When pushed to the limit by Bert, John began to check into irregularities in the latter's handling of the partnership accounts and sale of stock in the new company to outsiders. The letters reveal Hubbard's willingness to distort the truth, to ignore the needs of others, and to relish the grand gesture when it served his purpose. When John refused to sign a "cutthroat clause" that would have required full payment in case of any default in interest, Hubbard accused John of being "needlessly harsh" and offered to surrender. At this time, John had learned of Bert's affair with Alice Moore and the duplicity of his life in Cambridge. John's letter in reply, dated November 15, 1894, states in strong terms the irreconcileable break between the two men and is revealing of the character of both:

> *. . . last January, when the agreement containing the objectionable clause was presented for my signature, I refused point blank to sign it until it was changed to apply only to default of interest, notwithstanding a law suit had been entered and was apparently ready to go on. Did I fear your vengeance and hatred then? No, nor do I now. You cannot do, even at your worst but little harm and that only such as can be measured by dollars and cents. I wish I could say you had done no worse for yourself and others whom all the laws of nature demand you should cherish and protect. I have not asked you to "surrender" one iota; simply that the dates of payment be made so that I might be reasonably sure of being able to meet them when due, and that the "cut throat" clause be eliminated as to a default on payment of the principal of any of the notes, i.e. to read the same as the previous one dated Januy 2/94. This does not compare with the **harshness***

*of your **demand**. I know what you can do just as well as you do, if it suits your pleasure, flatters your vanity or gratifies your selfishness—now that you have a little season of power—this is your opportunity, upon the pretext of a refusal of your demands. You know full well that it will be impossible for me to raise the $6500.00 in addition to the $2,000.00 coming due Jany. 10th which I intend and expect to pay. I have not been able to repay the $1000. borrowed to pay you last July. Therefore you will have no more opportune time to apply harsh measures. If you see fit to carry out the implied threat, twill be but another milestone in our pathway of the last few years, and this one as was the last, a direct result of my response to your, "John you see what I want to do, can you help me." Almost every day I receive reminders of the treachery of 1892. Of course you know that after the "Lightening flash" which came a year ago last July, without the least intimation to me at any time that you thought of having a claim against me, I began quietly to search into your conduct first in connection with the business and then otherwise. Evidence multiplied until there could be no doubt. My surprise, pain and sorrow was like that caused by the "smashing of Idols." Do you wonder that I feared to trust myself to meet you at Gerot's, or on Friday, Nov 2nd? I had hoped nothing would ever occur to lead me to discuss this subject with anyone, believing it would be better that Bertha nor Frank should ever learn of it, at least from me, however, there is a limit to human endurance and sometimes while smarting under a keen sense of wrong human nature must give way or serious results follow. Bear in mind this is not written in a threatening spirit, but simply to explain some things which you attribute to "malice and hate."*
With kindly sorrow
John[11]

Bert was soon to return to Bertha and there would be a period of calm in East Aurora before the great scandal of 1902. The Roycroft venture began to succeed, and Elbert Hubbard was becoming a well known public figure and popular lecturer. Frank, who had been considerably shaken by her adored brother's behavior, could visit the family and her parents in East Aurora in the knowledge that all had been forgiven. The birth of a daughter to Bertha and Bert on January 5, 1896 seemed to offer the final proof of Bert's return to the fold. John would make his settlement with his brother-in-law in 1897 with a letter and check dated "Nov. 8 '97."He writes with his usual good will and attention to detail:

> *Learning that you are building and thinking that like all others placed in that position, you could use some money, I have made arrangements to anticipate the note which falls due in January and, therefore, send you herewith my check for $1818.76 Kindly return the note and assignment of life insurance, also the enclosed receipt duly signed. I am glad to see the evidence of prosperity attending your efforts.*[12]

With recovery from the Panic of '93 and the increase in sales, John realized that the plant must be expanded if the business was to keep pace with the demand. On April 27, 1895, the Directors authorized the President to "contract for the erection of a six story building on the lot in rear of the present building and fronting on Carroll Street."[13] The company purchased frontage on Carroll Street, arranged with Schmitt Bros, "honest builders,"[14] to purchase for $400.00 and tear down the abandoned New York Central Railroad station at William Street. Schmitt Bros. used the bricks from the station in the construction of "the first Larkin Building C., sixty by a hundred-and-fifty feet, six stories high, wood joists and floors, cast iron columns."[15] During the next five years new buildings were added as fast as possible. Frame construction was abandoned and replaced entirely with brick, steel and concrete construction. John, who had lived through the Great Fire in Chicago, was determined to provide the safest and healthiest environmant for his workers. John loved the process of building, the planning with the architects and builders, the contact with the workmen on the site, and he always demanded the best in workmanship and materials. Some of his happiest moments were spent overseeing the expansion of the works. The building boom continued until 1906, when the Frank Lloyd Wright Administration building (A building) was completed. There would be one more large expansion in 1912, when the big warehouse (R, S, and T buildings) was built.

John and Bert were not the only members of the family active in the business during these years. In these early days, Frank took a lively interest whenever her household and maternal duties permitted. Sometime in 1894 she served as a model in an advertisement. Posing, book in hand, she gave just the right touch of leisured elegance to the Chautauqua Spring Rocking and Reclining Chair.[16] The cut made from the photograph was used in the 18-page booklet offering a selection of products and a list of 10 premiums to choose from sent out probably in 1895. This brochure, apparently addressed to young people as well as adults, bore the title "Can We Break The Crust?" and carried on its cover a drawing by Palmer Cox of the then popular "Brownies."[17] This cartoon cover reflects John's (and probably his children's) delight in Cox's Brownies. Around the same time John even published under the company's name a reprint of one of Cox's popular collections with the wonderful title "Queerie Queers with Horns, Wings and Claws."[18]

Frank not only served the business as a model. Sometime before 1890, she had tried her hand at writing advertising copy for Clover Pink sachet powder which was to become one of the company's best selling products. What she wrote reveals her love of elegance and history:

> *There never was an age (or time) when perfume was so much used as at present, although in the seventeenth century perfumed powder which is now known as sachet powder was extensively used in the French court. . .before the famous Rambouillet circle met the Salon bleu used to be perfumed by sprinkling deliciously scented powder over plates of live coals. There is a daintiness from the scent of sachet powder that one seldom gets from a liquid perfume. It is considered vulgar and poor taste to use a strong or marked perfume. J.D. Larkin & Co,'s clover pink is delicate, refined and lasting.[19]*

The appeal of the glamour of French names was as popular in the cosmetic industry then as it is today, and it is easy to imagine Bert and his sister having fun with the game. For instance, J. D. Larkin & Co. became "parfumeurs" in 1884. Before that in 1878, a slinger introducing "Creme Oatmeal" soap has English on one side and French on the other, making a special offer of a box of 18 bars for $1.00 as "Notre Ontroduction." Clearly there was more enthusiasm than erudition involved.

By 1892, when Bert announced his intention to leave the company, John and Frank were faced with many concerns on the home front. There was the problem of the older children's education. Charlie was 17, Daisy 16 and John Jr. 15. John himself had had to cut short his schooling at an early age to go to work. He learned the soap business from the ground up, and he had attended Bryant and Stratton Business School, but he must have felt the lack of more formal training. Frank, on the other hand, was a graduate of the Normal College in Normal, Illinois, which her sisters had also attended. Frank's father Silas Hubbard had studied medicine at Castleton, Vermont and become a doctor. Her uncle, Solomon Hubbard, had studied law and was a prominent judge in Genesee County. Education was a matter of primary importance to both John and Frank, and they were anxious for the boys, at least, to have a college education.

In the fall of 1892, Charlie was enrolled in St. John's Military School in Manlius, N.Y., where, with five other boys from Buffalo, he was one of 123 boarding cadets. He appears in a picture in the 1893 *Annual* as a member of the Mendelssohn Club, a strikingly handsome boy in his cadet uniform, poised to make music on his banjo.[20] Tuition at the time was $550, and there were other expenses for uniforms and books. John kept copies of letters that he wrote between 1892 and 1894 to Colonel Verbeck, the Headmaster. On November 21, 1892 he sent a check for $11.00 to pay for Charlie's saber and belt. John lost no opportunity to make a sale, and the Colonel must have been impressed with the Combination Box and Chautauqua desk offer, because, on February 6, 1893, John writes to the Colonel:

Your favor of recent date enclosing check for $10.00 was duly recd. and placed to your credit in full of acct. Hope the Soap and Desk have been recd. and found satisfactory. Herewith find N. Y. check $262.63 in settlement of your bill dated Jany. 12/93. I am,
  Sincerely yours
  J.D. Larkin[21]

In the fall of 1893, John and Frank decided to send John Jr. to St. John's as well. However, the happy situation suggested in John's letter and in the 1893 *Annual* apparently did not persist. In December there was some trouble about a letter that Charlie wrote to his mother. For some reason the letter was withheld by the authorities, and John wrote to Col. Verbeck asking for a verbatim copy of the letter and to be informed ". . . if he has in any way broken or infringed the rules of the school. I make these requests because I want to fully understand all of the circumstances in connection with this matter."[22] The Colonel's reply must have been satisfactory, for on December 15, John sent a check for $248.00 to cover John Jr.'s bill and extended "the compliments of the season."[23] The boys would have returned home for Christmas, when they would have been able to lay their case before their father in person. Whatever the trouble may have been, we will never know. More than likely the restraints of military life went against the free spirited Larkin/Hubbard grain. In any case, John wrote January 10, 1894, to settle his accounts with the school and advise the Colonel: "I have concluded not to send the boys back to school this term." [24]

The effect of the 1893 depression was probably not a factor in this decision, though John was having a serious cash flow problem by 1894. Nevertheless he continued arrangements for the boys' schooling. One of Uncle Solomon Hubbard's daughters was married to Dr. F.D. Blakeslee who taught at Cazenovia Seminary, in Cazenovia, N.Y.[25] and from the letters we learn that John Jr., at least, attended Dr. Blakeslee's school for a time. Perhaps both boys were there during the 1894 school year. Charlie was a freshman at Lafayette College in the fall of 1895, and John's letter dated November 19, 1895, reveals that John Jr. was about to terminate his schooling with Dr. Blakeslee. It seems clear that John Jr. had difficulty applying himself to his studies, and his father had told him that "unless he showed good progress he would have to come home and go to work."[26] John and Frank had agreed that it would be better for the boy to be at home "where we can look after him every day."[27] It seems probable that Johnnie did return home, and that he may even have worked at the company in some capacity for a time. On January, 1896, he and Harry attended the annual stockholders meeting for the first time. Harry was attending "Cap" Mellon's school in Buffalo (later Lafayette High School), and a year later John Jr. was enrolled at Lafayette College where he remained for only two terms (1896–1897). John Jr. was finally fully employed at the company in 1898.

From the beginning John had wanted the business to be a family affair. He was anxious to have his boys share in the management of the company as soon as possible. Charlie was elected a director of the Larkin Soap Mfgr. Company at the time that Elbert Hubbard resigned in January of 1893. He was a student at St. John's at the time with four years of college ahead of him. The Minutes of the company show that he attended Director's meetings whenever he was home from school, as well as attending stockholders' meetings. Education was important, but a role in the family business was equally so. The only time that I can find a record of John's receiving a defeat in the matter of declaring a dividend occurred at the Directors' meeting July 5, 1894. The business showed a profit of $10,027.66, and John proposed a 2 percent dividend. The motion lost by three votes: John and Charlie in favor, the Coss brothers and D. D. Martin against. The motion was reintroduced a week later and passed, but John was anxious to build insurance against a recurrance. He wanted his boys at his side.

The problem of education, of course, was not limited to the boys. In 1895, Daisy was nineteen and attending St. Agnes School in Albany. Her stay at St. Agnes was to have great significance for the future. There she was to meet Annie Halderman, whose father, a career diplomat, once held the post of Minister to the court of Siam. Annie would be a life long friend and travelling companion to both Daisy and her mother. There, too, she met Alice Whitin, whose wealthy New England family gave their name to Whitinsville, Massachusetts. Charlie fell in love with his sister's friend, and he and Alice would be married in 1899, as soon as he graduated from Lafayette.

By 1895, the economy had begun to recover from the depression of '93, and the Larkin Soap Mfgr. Company in particular was enjoying success. John no longer had to consider selling his property on Hodge Avenue in order to meet the demands for payment that seemed to spring up on every side. In the next five years, the business would increase its sales five-fold from $1,058,187 in 1896 to $5,920,493 in 1901. The period was one of constant struggling to keep up with the demand for products and premiums. Real estate had to be acquired quickly and economically. John even had his cousin Tom Preston in New Jersey bid on property for him to keep the neighbors from taking advantage of the burgeoning business.[29] Buildings were razed and new ones built at a record rate. How gratifying this outward sign of success must have been to John with his passion for building: an outward and visible sign of the reward of industry, integrity and patience. From the farm in East Hamburg to the bright and bustling offices on Seneca Street had been a long but rewarding journey.

The decade of the '90s was not all smooth sailing, however, on the domestic front. As we have seen there were ups and downs with the children's education. John's letters reveal, too, that Frank was often in poor health. He never says much, but the accumulative effect of recurring reports that "Frank is very poorly now,"[30] and his writing to a doctor in New York for a "'Health Pamphlet' on the subject Hot Water Treatments"[31] suggest that Frank was not well. To what extent her problem was physical and to what extent emotional would be hard to say. Her history of "the Blues" before marriage might suggest the latter. In either case, she never seemed to regain her earlier strength after the loss of Edith and the baby Hubbard.

In addition to his concern for Frank's health, John was beset by anxieties for his two remaining siblings, Levi Larkin and Mary Weller. Levi, as he grew older, became even less dependable. In 1886, when he wrote to John for advice on the manufacture of soap, John wrote warning him of the difficulties of trying to make and sell soap on his own and generously offered to provide him with soap at less than cost.[32] There is no indication what Levi's response to this may have been. He was married to a fine woman, Eva Stark, and they had four children, but Levi could never settle down to anything. Sometime before 1888, he and Eva had gone to Florida, where he settled in Mount Dora. He had written John and apparently asked him to invest in some way to help Levi in the orange growing business. John's reply asks a number of questions that reflect his knowledge of farming and expresses a willingness to consider the investment if he can hope for a reasonable return:

> *I want to and find I must invest where returns will come from it, or at least where it will take care of itself until it can within a reasonable time make something for me. Frank wishes me to say that if you can send us a few Palms now, small ones, they would not be likely to get injured by the frost. . . Frank has been quite ill, but we are all pretty well now.*[33]

Levi replied to John on April 23d, sent a map of the property and announced that he was coming north and needed work. John replied May 3d suggesting that he could take orders for the company, and expressing willingness to help Levi, but that he could only do so in a limited way. There are no further letters until September of 1890, when John sent some money to Eva and informed her that her husband had not been at work for two months and they had had to fill his position at the works. The next letter, sent to Detroit, indicates that Levi has been trying to "sling" soap there without success. John urges him to find some kind of work—shoveling snow, taking care of furnaces, looking after lawns in summer, "anything to make an honest living. You don't want to get discouraged, there is something for everyone to do who is willing and determined to work."[34] Levi did not reply.

Levi apparently returned to Eva in Florida. Things went better. Eva took orders for Larkin soap and Levi must have applied himself to growing oranges, for he sent John and Frank a barrel of oranges in the spring of 1892.[35] On January 20th, 1895, Eva wrote to John in great distress. There is no exact account of what happened, but the story handed down in the family is that Levi, armed with a loaded gun, walked into the lake and fired off the gun. Whether the shooting was threatening to his family, to himself or to anyone else is not clear, but John's reply to Eva indicates that he was arrested and that the incident created quite a stir in the little community. John is sure that his brother was insane at the time of the incident, urges that he be examined by a physician and that he "should be given a fair chance in the trial to have this subject of his condition fully brought out." John offers Eva every help that he can, but lets her know that the hard times of the past years have left him considerably in debt. Should she wish to come north, he will help in every way he can to find a position for her. He refers to the severe winter in Florida causing severe losses.

Sometimes it seems as if everything about us joined forces to overcome us in our struggles to improve our condition, and I am glad to note in your letters a tone of hopefulness and a determination to keep on trying, perserverance with good judgement and health is almost sure to succeed.[36]

Levi was placed in an institution, and Eva and the children moved to a house in Eustis. Frank and John sent money, clothing and "things" to tide them over till some permanent arrangement could be made. John repeatedly stressed the importance of keeping the children with their mother. In June Eva was able to move west to Des Moines, Iowa, where she could be near a brother. John helped her financially with the move, and he and Frank continued to send things for the children and money to help with their education. Levi was not destined to remain long in the institution. John wrote to his mother in North Evans that on October 12 he was "taken with a bilious attack, did not seem to suffer much pain at any time but on the 27th passed quietly away."[37]

The depression of 1893, his problems with Bert, the sad career of his brother Levi and his wife's poor health were not the only problems John had to face in the '90s. There was his sister Mary. When she and Justus Weller separated John urged her to settle with Weller for $5,000 for herself and Weller's pledge to provide for their younger daughter, Nellie. Hattie, the older girl, was already married to Mr. F. R. Getman of Chicago. It is difficult to piece together the events that followed the separation, and there is no clear indication of its cause other than extreme incompatibility and, perhaps, Mary's instability. There is no suggestion of another woman in the case, but Weller had moved his business to Detroit (Levi worked for him there at one time), and Mary remained in Chicago.

The story of John's involvement with Mary's troubles begins probably at least ten years after the separation. Weller has not succeeded in the soap business and has tended to blame his troubles on John's success. In a letter to Mary, John answers Jus' charge that John did him in:

> . . . *the simple facts in the case are that he could not + did not adopt new methods of selling his goods. . . and his dishonesty in making the quality of his goods so poor his agents could not sell them fast enough to make it pay them, are the consequences of his poor luck + not doing well in business, + now he tells this pitiful story to shirk the responsibility of providing for you and Nellie, and is just what he intended doing in the first place. I understood he had gone into the Livery business + out of the soap business entirely.*[38]

In another place, John tells her that Jus has been in Florida for some months. Was he perhaps with Levi? Finally, Jus drops out of sight. Little is known of his whereabouts until Frank records in her diary of that date that he died in Detroit on January 14, 1901.

It is clear from the letters that Mary had serious mental health problems as well as financial problems. Before 1888, John had tried to provide a home for her in North Evans with their mother and William. Mary had come to Buffalo with her younger daughter Nellie, and the venture had been a complete failure. Mary was querulous and demanding; her mother, over seventy and already burdened with the care of William, became ill under the strain; and John had to insist that Mary and Nellie return to Chicago. In December of 1888, Mary wanted to return to Buffalo and live with her mother. In correspondence with Mary's elder daughter, Hattie, John felt obliged to refuse this request with a flat no. Then in 1890, Nellie dropped a bombshell by getting married after what Hattie termed a "clandestined courtship." John's reply is characteristically quiet and cool headed: "If Nellie is married I hope for her sake that her husband will prove to be a good man, and do not see why your mother should be at all upset."[39] By November of 1890, Mary's mental condition had worsened to the point where neither of the girls could care for her. John writes asking if Hattie has written to her father. With the pressures that he is under, John cannot undertake to provide for his sister. He suggests a home of some kind where she can be looked after. The Victorian terms sound particularly grim to us—The Old Ladies Home ɔr The Home for Incurables. These places offered the only refuge for the mentally and physically ill, the equivalent of today's nursing homes. Arrangements were made to place Mary in The

Home for Incurables, and John offered to pay half of the expense of the home and provide for Mary's clothing.

Mary went to the home and John kept his part of the bargain, sending money as needed and supplying clothing and the money to cover dressmaker's fees. John's letter to Hattie expressing his hopes for Mary is characteristic, reminiscent of his response to Frank's complaint of the Blues years before. John's healthy, direct, methodical mental processes simply could not imagine the tortured complexities of the neurotic psyche:

> *Trusting that she will realize how much her comfort depends on her own actions and upon a disposition to make the best of everything around her, and that she will see the necessity of trying to do something no matter how simple and plain, to take up her attention, speaking kind words of appreciation to those around her, she will be surprised to see how much difference it will make and how much happiness such things will develop every day.*[40]

Again in a similar vein, he wrote to Mary about the loss of a watch she had pawned:

> *I cannot send the money to redeem it, I am sorry you have to lose it, just bear in mind that we have our cares and responsibilities to meet every day, and often the demands seem to require more than we can do. Be cheerful as you can and do not worry about what you cannot help.*[41]

Matters went on in this way, Mary complaining and being miserable, accusing him of neglect, never able to accept the reality of her situation. The poor woman was sick, and John knew it. With his responsibilities to his family and his business, he could not afford to be sucked into the maelstrom of her neurosis. The last straw came when some of her friends in Chicago saw fit to put Mary on a train for Buffalo, unaccompanied and helpless. John's letter to F. R. Getman gives the details:

> *. . . I am in no way responsible for Mrs. Weller except so far as I have been compelled to assume the payment of her board by her friends ? in Chicago placing her on the cars with a ticket to Buffalo, thus leaving her to take care of herself while en route or to the tender mercies of entire*

strangers. When she arrived one eye was black and blue
caused by a fall in trying to take care of herself... She begged
hard to go and see her Mother if only for a few days, and
promised to make no trouble or work for her Mother. I
explained to her as I did to the missionary who lived in your
house, that Mother was 75 years old and not able to do much,
but she forgot all about it and kept Mother awake nights until
she was taken very ill and the doctor told me that Mrs. Weller
must be taken away if we wanted Mother to live. . . We
inquired of different Physicians for a place to take her but
could find none and the Providence Retreat was the only one
suggested by anyone of them. Mrs. Weller has not developed
symptoms of being dangerous to anyone, that I know of. I
was compelled to take her there because there was no better
place here that she could be taken to. If her children want
her to come to them and will take care of her I have no
objection whatever, but think some promise and guaranty
should be given that she will not be shipped about the
country alone for she is not in a condition to take care of
herself anywhere. [42]

John asks if Hattie could come for her mother, speaks of the cash demands on him that have brought him almost to despair, but promises to do what he can to help with the expenses of returning Mary to Chicago. Here the entries in the letter book, the only source we have for Mary's story, end. The date and place of her death are unknown, although Harry H. Larkin Jr. has a note in the MS genealogy that he compiled that Mary "died with her daughter Hattie." Nellie, Mary's younger daughter, had been married in 1890, as mentioned above, to a Mr. Joachim and moved to Lincoln Nebraska. John's children, Ruth, Harry and Frances (Daisy), contributed to her support for many years after she was widowed. As late as 1960, she was still living, and her granddaughter wrote a letter for her to her cousin Ruth Larkin Robb thanking her for "your kind letter and that blessed check." In the letter are several revealing references to Mary Durant Larkin and her son William:

Uncle Willie had that Locomotor Ataxia as you thought
and also had both ankles broken trying to walk one time. He
was a dear suffering soul and very unhappy. But our dear

grandmother was very courageous and always had her Bible on the table, many times open.[43]

John met the various vicissitudes of business and family that marked the 1890s with his characteristice calm and acceptance. On the whole the decade was a time of healing and growth, a busy and productive time for all the family. Furthermore, it was during the 1890s that the family discovered the delights of travel. Frank, in her diaries and journals provides a wealth of detail of these family travels and gives us glimpses of England and Europe at the turn of the century. Her involvement in the social and intellectual life of the city meant a great deal to Frank, and in travel she found much to enrich that life. Above all, however, she found peace of mind and release from the "blues" that plagued her always.

---

[1] Martin Diary, July 29, 1885.

[2] Jack Quinan, "Elbert Hubbard's Roycroft," *Head, Heart and Hand: Elbert Hubbard and the Roycrofters*, Rochester, NY: University of Rochester Press, 1994, p.11.

[3] "The Forum Extra," June 1890, D. D. Martin Collection, SUNY Buffalo Archives.

[4] Martin, letter to Crate Larkin November 3, 1924.

[5] Ibid.

[6] Ibid.

[7] Martin, Card Memo, initially dated 10/15/03 and continued thereafter, BECHS Darwin R. Martin Collection.

[8] Martin, *Autobiography*, pp. 175,176.

[9] BECHS Archives, Larkin Company Inc. Records. In exchange for 1,300 shares Larkin Soap Mfg. Co.'s capital stock, valued at $26,000, Hubbard received 13 shares of Hyde Park Land Syndicate stock, valued at $9,000; 40 shares of Delaware Parkside Co. stock valued at $6,500; and 3 promisory notes, two for $4,000 due January 1st and July 1st, 1993, and one for $2,500 due January1st, 1894. Martin and others give considerably higher figures, but to date this is all I have been able to document.

[10] Martin, *Autobiography*, p. 170.

[11] BECHS Archives, JDL LCB, pp. 242–245.

[12] BECHS Archives, Larkin Company, Inc. Records.

[13] BECHS Archives, Larkin Soap Manufacturing Company, Minutes, p. 29.

[14] Martin. *Autobiography*, p.183

[15] Ibid. p.184.

[16] BECHS Archives, Larkin Company, Inc. Records, copy in the author's collection.

[17] The only copy of this booklet that I have seen is in the private collection of Jerome P. Puma, who graciously supplied me with a copy.

[18] The Buffalo and Erie County Library Rare Book Room has a copy of this book. Could it have been offered as a premium?

[19] MS in FHL's hand, BECHS Archives, Larkin Company, Inc Records

[20] *St. John's Military School Annual, 1893*, Manlius, N.Y., p. 26.

[21] JDL LCB, p. 192.

[22] JDL LCB, December 2, 1893, p. 221.

[23] Ibid. p. 224.

[24] Ibid. p. 227.

[25] Dr. Blakeslee served as President of Cazenovia College from 1900 to 1908.

[26] Ibid. p. 176. Loose letter addressed to Dr. Blakeslee dated Buffalo N.Y., November 19, 1895.

[27] Ibid.

[28] Lafayette College, *Biographical Record* information supplied to me by Cyrus S. Fleck, Jr., Registrar, in a letter dated April 22, 1994.

[29] JDL LCB loose letter to Thomas Preston, 10/30/1895.

[30] JDL to Dr. Blakeslee, 12/18/1895, LCB, p. 281.

[31] JDL letter to Dr. A. Wilford Hall, 1/11/1896, LCB, p.282.

[32] JDL letter to Levi H. Larkin, 2/25/1886, LCB, p. 15.

[33] JDL letter to Levi H. Larkin, 3/8/1888, LCB, p. 90.

[34] JDL letter to Levi H. Larkin, 12/16/1890, LCB, p. 131.

[35] JDL to Levi H. Larkin, 4/9/1892, LCB, p. 173.

[36] JDL to Eva Larkin, 2/10/1895, LCB, p. 254.

[37] JDL to Mary Larkin Hoag, 11/5/1895, LCB, loose letter.

[38] JDL to Mary L. Weller, 9/29/1888, LCB, p. 98.

[39] JDL to Hattie Getman, 7/10/1890, LCB, p. 119.

[40] JDL to Hattie Getman, 11/26/1890, LCB, p. 129.

[41] JDL to Mary Weller, 4/11/1891, LCB, p. 145.

[42] JDL to F.R. Getman, 7/27/1895, LCB, p. 264–265.

[43] Nellie Joachim, to Ruth Larkin Robb, OL 3/4/1960, in author's collection.

Chapter 6

New Horizons 1890-1900

During the decade of the 1890s the Larkin Soap Mfg. Co. was growing from a relatively small manufacturing and mail order company into one of the largest companies of its kind not only in Buffalo, but in the country. The vigorous advertising and soliciting of customers throughout the country, the immense popularity of the premium offers with the Combination Box and the insistance on quality at the lowest possible cost to the customer brought a flood of orders that threatened to swamp the modest soap company on Seneca Street. The simple matter of keeping track of thousands of orders in the clumsy old ledgers that John Larkin and young Darwin Martin had labored over in the early days was mind boggling. But Darwin was a very bright young man. He observed the card catalog files in which the books at the library were listed, and he realized that a card file system could be the solution to the problem. He tells the story himself in his pamphlet published in 1932:

> Beginning in OCTOBER 1886, with the first shipment from FACTORY TO FAMILY, the first ledger cards were made, and then began, I believe, THE FIRST CARD-LEDGER IN THE WORLD. . . I think the card-ledger was born in the Larkin office, and the fact deserves its honored place in future encyclopedias.[1]

One problem that faced the company was that of raising capital in order to keep pace with the demands for merchandise and the expansion of the plant. In January of 1892, a form letter was drawn up and sent out to established customers offering them the opportunity to purchase stock in the new company. The idea behind this move was to establish the company on a new basis, that of a co-operative relationship between the producer of goods and the consumer. The letter read in part: "We have long believed in this principle that underlies all co-operative industries, viz: that the producer and the consumer should join hands, and that the faithful employe and the loyal patron should share justly in the benefits which they have helped to create."[2]

The letter was signed John D. Larkin, President. A similar letter followed in May of 1892, offering one share of stock for $10.00—"and we will give you gratis a desk or a lamp."[3] John, as President, spoke of the success of the "cooperative plan" of obtaining a large number of stockholders when the stockholders of the new company met January 19, 1893. The next few years brought hard times with the panic of '93, but, as we have seen, the company weathered that storm well and came out under full sail as she headed for the turn of the century.[4]

As the business grew and prospered, the number of products and premiums increased and the requirements for manufacturing and storing them demanded the extensive building program referred to above. The company that had been manufacturing a dozen or so products—soap, perfume, sachet, and other household items—in 1890, offered several hundred products by 1900, and the premiums had increased from the initial ten Offered in "Can We Break the Crust?" to 339 in 1900. In 1893, total sales amounted to $476,159; in 1900, total sales were $5,357,243.

This rapid growth, of course, called for many changes in personnel. The number of employees in both the office and the plant increased dramatically. Together with the Coss brothers, Darwin Martin had acquired stock in the company and was made a director when the new company was formed in 1892. When Hubbard left, Martin acquired more stock and was elected to the position of Secretary/Auditor, but with little or no increase in salary. On December 8, 1895 he wrote a strong letter to John arguing that he should assume the position left vacant by Hubbard.[5] It was not until 1898, however, that he was granted the position of Secretary with a salary of $10,000. Perhaps John was wary of this young man's aggressive and ambitious nature and hesitated to give him too much rein.

It has been suggested that it was Martin's aggressiveness, in part, that prompted John to strengthen the position of the family in the management of the burgeoning business.[6] It was in 1898 that John persuaded his brother-in-law, William R. Heath to move to Buffalo from Chicago to head up a legal department for the company. In 1897, John employed a young New

Englander, Harold M. Esty, who had come to Buffalo to attend the Heathcote School on Delaware Avenue, run by his relatives, Mr. and Mrs. Clarence Wheeler. Harold and John's daughter, Daisy, met, fell in love, and were married in 1899. In 1898, John D. Jr., having spent a year at Lafayette College, was employed, and in 1899 Charles graduated from Lafayette and came to work as a chemist in the perfume laboratory. John's son Harry was also majoring in chemistry at Lafayette and would start work in the business on graduating in 1903. From the early days of the partnership with Bert, John had seen his business as a family affair, an enterprise that would provide for those closest and dearest to him.

The rapid growth of the business both provided for and required a new element in John's life, that of travel. With the increasing profits from the business after 1895, John was able to think of travel abroad both for recreational and for business purposes. His roots were in England, and he must have heard a lot about the Old Country from his mother as well as from Aunt Mary Balcom and the Durant relatives he visited in Winterbourne, Ontario. England was in his blood and bones. From a business point of view, he would have realised the value of personal contacts with the sources of essential oils used in the manufacture of his soaps and perfumes. John left no record of his travels abroad or of his business and personal contacts there. We do know, however, that it was recorded in the minutes of the company that the President would be absent for a few weeks in the spring of 1897, and that Charles was appointed to act as Treasurer at a salary of $10 per week.[7]

Frank, unlike her husband, kept diaries and scrapbooks that give considerable detail of their travels together.[8] Frank had travelled on her own to visit relatives in the mid-west. She had made visits to her parents in Hudson, Illinois, and in 1895 she travelled to Berea, Kentucky, to visit her widowed sister Daisy and her sons Frank and George. She suffered poor health for some time after that, and, perhaps on her doctor's advice, John decided that she should join him on his trip to England in 1897. On June 23 of that year, John and Frank sailed from New York on the *S.S. Saint Louis* for Southampton accompanied by Miss Berry, a trained nurse. Good friends from Buffalo, Mr. and Mrs. Spencer Kellogg, were also on the ship. Both families had daughters already travelling in the British Isles. Young Frances and Bessie Kellogg had preceded their parents for a tour of Ireland and Scotland and would meet the ship at Southampton. This certainly was Frank's first trip abroad, if not John's, and she anticipated it eagerly.

Miss Berry proved a congenial companion. They took their meals on deck whenever weather permitted, and were fascinated by the parade of distinguished passengers that passed before their steamer chairs. His Excellency The Right Hon. Sir Julian Pauncefote, G. C. B., British Ambassador to the United States and Lady Pauncefote, with four daughters, made a great impression on Frank. According to the passenger list the Ambassador and his family were accompanied by a maid, valet and footmen. In descending order the list consisted of assorted aristocrats and socialites, often accompanied by maids and valets, distinguished clergymen, including the Rev. Wallace Nutting of Providence and the Rev. Dr. Lubeck of New York, and members like themselves of the business and professional middle class. Frank's diary entries give a sense of her enthusiasm and the flavor of their days aboard ship:

> *June 24th, 1897*
> *We had breakfast on deck. It is so restful to sit in our steamer chairs and drift on and on. I opened my sister Mary's letter this morning and we were much touched by her kindness and affection. In the morning we saw a large school of porpoise which was quite exciting—also a ship in the distance. Had a little chat with Dr. Lubeck a New York Clergyman who has his meals on deck near us—and became acquainted with Madame Geoffroi . . . Sir Julian stopped in front of our chairs to chat with the mate. He is a tall and distingue looking old Englishman with white hair and mustache. Dr. Seward Webb is very interesting and stalks (not walks) the deck dressed in a dark blue suit of clothes, wears a black and white check cap and tie to match.*

> *June 25, 1897 Four Bells—P.M.*
> *Mr. Larkin and Miss Berry and myself are sitting on portside of deck. Miss B. and myself have all our meals on deck. The steward brings the menu card out, we choose what we like, and he brings our meals out in flat baskets divided into little compartments. Sat up in the bow a long time this morning. I had an unexpected letter from Bert (Elbert Hubbard) sent to the Purser to be delivered this morning. It seemed like hearing directly from Ruth and I was quite overcome.*

> *We passed two sailing vessels about twelve miles from*

us—could plainly see the colors through the glasses—also the smoke. I have read Elbert Hubbard's Rosa Bonheur *today, and loaned it to Madame Geoffroi. This afternoon we walked entirely around the deck. Saw Sir Julian sitting with one of his daughters on the starboard side. He was reading a new red covered book. Glancing at the title I saw* The New Rector. *Several Yale men on board with G. A. A on their caps. Watched the young men play quoits in the bow. The watch in the "crows nest" is most interesting. The man I saw today is so weatherbeaten that his face is a dark tan color.*

On Sunday, June 27th, John and Frank attended Sunday services held in the Dining Saloon (her first in two and a half years), and on the same day Frank notes the ethnic mix of the ship's passengers. "We have on board that we know Americans, English, French, Spaniards, German Jews, an African maid, and Mr. Larkin says in the second class he saw one Chinaman." There was a concert on the 28th. On the 29th it rained and Frank "took breakfast with Mr. Larkin in the dining saloon," but the weather cleared so they could have lunch and dinner on deck. On June 30th they arrived in Southampton, where daughter Frances and Bessie Kellogg met the boat. The pilot brought the mail bag on board, and the Larkins received a letter from Frances written from Ireland saying that she would stand on the wharf and wave her United States flag. An hour before they landed John was able "to see through his glasses three ladies standing apart and one was waving a small flag. I went to the bow with Miss Berry and waved our flag and distinctly saw Miss Stroud-Smith, Bessie and Frances." John and Mr. Kellogg were among the first passengers to land. After John and Miss Stroud-Smith (apparently the girls' travelling companion) had cleared customs, the party took a compartment and entrained for London, "and a very jolly party we were on the train!" Arriving at half past seven, they took two cabs and drove to the Hotel Metropole. Frank comments that "we saw many ladies and gentlemen in evening dress and everything and everybody very gay just after the Jubilee."

John had cousins who worked in a bank at 15 Lombard Street, a Mr. Harding and his son William. Next morning John and Frank and Frances took a "rubber tired cab" and drove about to see the Victoria Embankment, the Houses of Parliament, Westminster and St. Paul's cathedrals, Threadneedle Street, and the Bank of England, concluding their tour with a stop at the bank in Lombard Street where John introduced his cousins to his wife and daughter and arrangements were made for dinner that night at the Hotel Metropole with the Harding family. That evening Frank donned her pink tea gown and with John and Frances descended to a private drawing room where the Hardings were received and to which they retired after dinner for a visit that lasted until after ten o'clock. Miss Nellie Stroud-Smith joined the party after dinner. From Frank's diary it seems clear Miss Stroud-Smith is a member of the Harding family: "Mr. Larkin's relatives consist of Mr. Wm. Adolphus Harding, Mrs. Harding, Miss Harding, Miss Nellie, and Mr. Wm. Jr.."[9]

The next day there was more sightseeing this time "in a four wheeler with Miss Stroud-Smith and Mr. Larkin." Frank had expected London to be gray and smokey, and she was enchanted by the gay colors of the window boxes, the shop windows and the bright uniforms and fancy parasols she saw everywhere. That afternoon the Larkins left London for Leamington, Warwickshire, and the tour of the English countryside. From Leamington there were excursions to Warwick Castle, Kenilworth and Stratford on Avon. Frank revelled in seeing the world that Bert had brought home to her in the *Little Journeys* and in the talks they must have had in East Aurora after his return to Bertha and the Roycroft. On the 4th of July, "we decorated our room with U. S. flags and had strawberries and roses in our room." Frank and Miss Berry stayed in the hotel while John and Frances travelled to London again and returned with presents. On the 9th of July they went on to Chester where they took a carriage out to see the walls, visited the Cathedral, and John and Frances visited a book shop and bought photographs and a red leather-bound prayer book for Frank. One day Frank was indisposed with a headache, and John and Frances walked across the River Dee and into Wales where they visited Eaton Park, the estate of the Duke of Westminster. Everywhere that he went John took many pictures with his camera, and the photographs remain a clear record of their adventures to this day. Before they left Chester, John hired a guide and he and Frances "went around the entire wall." Frank comments that she is "not strong enough to do this."

They left Chester on the 12th of July and went north to Liverpool by train. Basket luncheons were handed in to the carriage en route, and the travellers arrived refreshed at their hotel where they were shown to a third floor room with a sea breeze. Frank drove out with John in her first Hansom Cab to do a little shopping before dinner. Next day there were more visits to shops to order gowns for Frances, and Frank was much impressed by the sales girls: "In the cloak and dressmaking departments, the sales women

92

are tall, have good figures, dress in black silk or satin plainly but beautifully made and have the manner and bearing of ladies."

From Liverpool the party proceeded to Furness Abbey in Lancashire where they stayed in a beautiful hotel situated on the Abbey grounds adjacent to the ruins. That evening they were entertained at dinner at the Vicarage by the Reverend Mr. Frederick Harding and his wife, another of John's Harding connections. Frank, who was enchanted by the romantic associations of the Abbey, spent many happy hours among the ruins and in the surrounding countryside. Mr. Turner, the Abbey guide, picked flowers for her from the stones of the ruin and told her the seeds had been given to him to plant in the crevices by John Ruskin.

On the morning of the 16th, after breakfast with the Hardings at the Abbey and last photographs taken and goodbyes said, the Larkins left on the 10 o'clock train for Edinburgh. It rained in Edinburgh, as it is wont to do, but the travellers managed to take in all the sights and to do some shopping. They visited John Knox's home and the Castle, where the soldiers were drilling and where Frances had seen the celebration of the Queen's Jubilee a short time before.

On the night of the 22nd, they took the sleeper from Edinburgh to London. They slept well, and enjoyed the attentions of the Scots porter who brought them tea and a plate of biscuits before the train arrived at Eustace Station at seven in the morning. They again stayed at the Hotel Metropole where they were joined by the Kellogg family. The two days before heading for Southampton and home were spent seeing the National Gallery with Frances as a guide, attending a short service at Westminster Abbey and shopping. Frank devotes several pages to the National Gallery where she saw for the first time works of Rosa Bonheur, Rembrandt, Reynolds, Michelangelo and Turner. Her comments on the students she observed in the Gallery foreshadow her interest in and support of her nephew George Carlock's career in art and perhaps suggest a sense of something lacking in her own life:

I think I was as much interested in the students as the pictures. Some women with their gowns covered with red aprons were between fifty and sixty years old and as rapt and interested as any of the younger artists. This is what makes life worth living—to be really interested—intensely so if you can—in doing and accomplishing something—but

> *the hopes, fears, aspirations, jealousies and heartaches of being just an artist—and not being a great artist.*[10]

The trip to England ended all too soon after several days sightseeing around Southampton with John, photographing the birthplace of Dr. Watts, the great hymnist, and gathering armfuls of heather and broom. It was a source of great satisfaction to John to see his beloved Frank so delighted with England. She might never be strong, but she would always thrive on travel, and his greatest delight was to provide everything to make this possible. The Kellogg family arrived in due course, and on the 24th of July they all boarded the German ship *Bremen* bound for New York. The crossing was rougher than before: Frank was confined to her stateroom during some rough weather, and there was heavy fog off Newfoundland. The voyagers were glad to see New York's beautiful harbor and to return to home and family.

On this first trip abroad, Frank discovered the true panacea for her physical and emotional troubles. She was never happier than when traveling. Over the next decade, until the outbreak of World War I, the Larkins went frequently to England and Europe in the early summer. In 1898, they took the children with them: Charles, Frances, John Jr., Harry and Ruth. Crossing to Liverpool in mid June, they travelled to London where they renewed their contacts with relatives and friends. John had business with the essential oil people in France, and they travelled through Holland on the way to Paris, then back to London, sailing from Liverpool for New York on July 23, Cunard Line, *S. S. Lucania*. Frank made special note in her scrapbook of two prominent passengers aboard the *Lucania*: Cornelius Vanderbilt, millionaire head of the New York Central Railroad, returning from Europe after a year recuperating from a stroke; and Richard Croker, the powerful Tammany boss who ruled his political associates with a hand of iron.

The two powerful men, one broken in health and the other impressively robust, would have presented to Frank a sharp contrast to the character of her unassuming, considerate and loving John, who was himself rapidly becoming a "Captain of Industry." Characteristic of his quiet love of fun is the post card that John mailed to Frank from Paris addressed to their home on Hodge Avenue in Buffalo:

> *de la Tour Eiffel, le 8th July 1898*
> *Dear Frank,*

94

Having a few minutes time here I take pleasure in wishing
you a Bon Voyage and safe return to your home.
Sincerely yours
John D. Larkin[11]

John must have anticipated with pleasure her delight when they reached home on receiving the card that her husband had sent her from Paris. There was still in the man of business a touch of the "Adolphus Green-Pickle" of their courting days.

Again in the summer of 1899, John and Frank took the children to Europe, but this time without Frances, who, as we shall see, had been married to Harold M. Esty in June. Charlie, just graduated from Lafayette College and engaged to be married, joined the family. On June 11th they sailed from New York on the White Star liner *Cymric*. This time they made a considerable tour of the Continent. After a stop in London and a visit with friends in England, they crossed from Dover to Calais. The itinerary consisted of the circuit south from Paris to Dijon; thence east to Geneva, Lausanne, Berne, Lucerne; north through Basel, Colmar and Strassgurg to Wiesbaden; then through Coblentz and Cologne and west to Brussels, Ghent, and finally Ostend to Dover and back to London. Frank's scrapbook bears witness that this was a happy family excursion. Somewhere in Germany, Charlie had a postcard made with his own handsome picture on one side to send home to his fiancee and friends. At the Maison Savino in Brussels, next to the Cook's Travel offices, Frank bought fine Belgian lace that would become a treasured family hierloom. The elegance of the name of the establishment is belied by the photograph that shows a small shop, its window hung with "real lace," at 43, Rue de la Madeleine. In Oxford Street, London, John purchased a copy of Walton's *Complete Angler* for 15 shillings. On August 19th the Larkins sailed from Southampton on the *Saint Louis* for New York and home. There is no record of any more trips abroad before 1907, although it seems likely that John, at least, travelled to England during that time on business for the Company and for his farms in Canada. But that gets us ahead of our story.

By 1890 John and Frank were becoming increasingly prominent in the business and social circles of Buffalo. John's position as a respected member of the business community grew as his company grew. His quiet but firm integrity, his deliberate good judgment, together with his positive attitude and his consideration for others won him the respect and affection of his fellow businessmen. His advice was sought, and at times his help. When

John Albright ran into financial difficulties and was unable to meet the cost of building his Art Gallery, John Larkin came to his rescue with a loan.[12] The banks in Buffalo soon recognized the value of John's financial acuity and sound judgment, and he was soon to serve as an officer of The Central National Bank of Buffalo and the Marine Midland Bank. Indeed, in 1905, as Vice President of the Central National, he put his signature on United States $5 and $10 bills, as was the custom when currency was still issued by banks.[13]

When the Ellicott Square Building was completed in 1896, the Ellicott Club, an association of business and professional men, took possession of the rooms that had been prepared for it in the "largest commercial office structure in the world."[14] Its chief aim was "to promote social intercourse among its members" and to "provide the members with a meeting place in the business portion of the said city."[15] Just when John Larkin joined this group is not certain. His name does not appear in the members handbook for 1898, but he is listed as a member in 1902. His position in the business community was firmly established by the turn of the century, and he would have known personally many of the members. The membership list for 1904 reads like a "Who's Who" of Buffalo's business community: Albright, Bissell, Clement, Coatsworth, Goodyear, Gratwick, Hamlin, Hengerer, Kellogg, Kleinhans, Knox, Larkin, Letchworth, Mack, Olmsted, Plimpton, Pratt, Rochester, Schoelkopf, Urban, Weed, Wendt, Wilcox and Yates, to name a few. The club occupied a number of rooms on the ground floor of the Ellicott Square building, all handsomely furnished and elegantly decorated. There were rooms available to members for meetings, no tipping was allowed, and smoking was forbidden in the main dining room and the ladies' rooms. There was a Ladies' Entrance on Washington Street, exclusively for ladies and the gentlemen accompanying them, and members could issue guest cards, printed or engraved, permanent or temporary, to ladies residing in their households which would give them the privilege of entertaining friends at the club. Frank undoubtedly availed herself of these privileges from time to time, but there is no written evidence.

After the move to Hodge Avenue in 1887, Frank found herself increasingly involved in Buffalo's social and intellectual circles. She was a woman of considerable intelligence and creative drive, and for all her bouts with ill health, she was never one to be idle while there was life to be lived. Frank was a leading member of a literary club whose members took turns presenting papers on various subjects. Meetings were held in the house on Hodge Avenue from time to time, and guest speakers were frequently invited. She became a member of the DAR chapter in Buffalo and developed a great interest in genealogy. She was also a member of the Twentieth Century Club, organized in 1896, and by 1905, she and John were members of the Buffalo Country Club. Among her close friends were the poet James N. Johnson and the artist Lars Sellstedt, a founder of the Buffalo Fine Arts Academy. Mrs. Folsom, whose niece, Frances Folsom, had married President Cleveland during his first term in office in 1886, had become quite fond of Frank, and on March 7, 1890, she invited her to a family luncheon at the Folsom home on Linwood Avenue. Frank, with her literary flair, left us in her notebook an account that shows a journalist's penchant for detail:

> *I have just taken lunch with Mrs. Grover Cleveland at her Aunt Mrs. Folsom's on Linwood Ave.—I had expected from all that I had heard and from her pictures to see a very lovely person—and was charmed with the unaffected almost girlish manner of this ex-president's wife. She is so free from all the little affectations of most society women, all her movements are so free and unstudied, that I·must confess I had to watch myself to keep from watching her. Tall, quite erect, a graceful head covered with an abundance of brown hair— worn pompadour in front and in a large high coil at the back—dark, clearly pencilled eyebrows, very frank sparkling clear grey eyes—rather small expressive mouth, red lips, a pretty, well-cut chin, handsome, rather large soft throat—this is the head and face of Frances Folsom Cleveland. Her hands are large but very well shaped and white— she wore today on her hands only her wedding ring. Her dress I should judge was her travelling costume and was of fawn colored cloth combined with a rich shade of brown velvet—at the neck was narrow pleated valenciennes lace, the collar was fastened by a dull Roman gold medallion pin—being an informal luncheon at one o'clock, no one except relatives present beside Mrs. Tabor, her son and myself—Mrs. Cleveland was very simply and elegantly dressed . . . tucked in her belt was a bunch of double purple violets. At the table she sat opposite me and had an appetite like any other healthy young woman. She spoke of her friend Mrs. Whitney who had just died—of the little baby she had left—then of the book* Lorna Doon *by Blackmur.*[16]

The last year of the century was marked by two weddings that brought major changes to the family. On June 7, 1899, Frances Elberta was married to Harold M. Esty in the family home at 125 Hodge Avenue. Harold had come from Framingham, Massachusetts, to attend the Heathcote School. He and Frances met, fell in love, and Harold was soon employed by his future father-in-law. On December 19, Charlie was married to Mary Alice Whitin of Whitinsville, Massachusetts, whom he had met through his sister at St. Agnes School in Albany

John and Frank like most proud parents determined to spare nothing in providing for the wedding of their eldest daughter, and the marriage was set to take place at seven o'clock in their home at 125 Hodge Avenue. The family had already left the Delaware Avenue Baptist Church in favor of St. Paul's Episcopal Cathedral, and the ceremony was to be conducted by the Rev. J. A. Regester of that parish. For weeks ahead Frank was busy seeing to arrangements with the dressmaker, the florists and the caterers. There were out of town guests to be looked after—some would be put up at the Lenox Hotel on North Street, others might stay with friends of the family. The guest list was limited to one hundred and fifty, family and close friends, and even that number must have taxed the facilities of the modest house on Hodge Avenue. The newspaper account is worth quoting for the picture it evokes of the period.

> *The house was decorated with a lavish arrangement of June flowerage, long stemmed American Beauties and jardinieres of white roses in the parlor, doorways framed with asparagus vines and bunches of white peonies tied with white satin ribbons. The hall in palms and peonies, and the library, where the ceremony was performed, massed at the back with tall palms and ferns, with vases of luxuriant pink roses. An orchestra stationed in the hall played the "Lohengrin" as the bridal party descended the staircase, the officiating clergyman, Rev. J. A. Regester of St. Paul's Cathedral, going first, followed by little Ruth Larkin, in a dainty white frock, wreath of daisies on her hair and carrying the bride's bouquet of lilies of the valley. The ushers, Mr. John D. Larkin Jr., Mr. Harry Hubbard Larkin, brothers of the bride, Mr. Elbert Hubbard, Jr., of East Aurora and Frank Carlock of Harrodsville, Ky., preceded the maid of honor, Miss Betsy Whitin of Whitinsville, Mass. who wore a costume of pale green silk with overdress of point d'esprit trimmed with filmy silvery ruchings of chiffon and crystal. The bride walked*

with her father, who gave her away. Mr. Charles H. Larkin
was the best man. The bride wore an exquisite gown of heavy
white satin with full court train, the front of the skirt orna-
mented with orange blossoms . . . The high coiffure was
finished with a shell comb worn by the great-great-grand-
mother of the bride, and the long sweeping tulle veil was
secured with a point lace butterfly.[17]

Frank, wearing a rich gown of white silk trimmed with black velvet and accompanied by Mrs. Whitin in plum colored silk and Miss [Alice] Whitin, in "a striking gown of blue satin bodice rimmed with jewels,"[18] and the groom's aunt, Mrs. Lester Wheeler, in grey silk, joined the bridal party at the foot of the stairs and moved into the library to Wagner's stately music. The ceremony over, "supper was served by Clark in a marquee on the lawn"[19] where the tables were tastefully decorated with maidenhair fern and pink roses.

The whole affair must have been a source of great satisfaction to John, the burgeoning industrialist, and his bride of twenty five years. Looking back over those years to the simple wedding in Dr. Hubbard's parlor in Hudson, Illinois, they must have felt that with all the struggle and heartbreak that the years had brought they had wrought well in building a family bound by ties of interest and affection. It was a happy, busy time. The summer lay before them: Charlie's graduation was just two weeks off, and then the trip to Europe. Dr. and Mrs. Hubbard would celebrate their 50th wedding anniversary in Hudson, Illinois on the 27th of September. Whether Frank travelled to Hudson is unknown, but she pasted a newspaper account of the event in her scrapbook, along with the commemorative poem that was read at the occasion and handsomely printed by the Roycroft Press. In December the family would travel to Whitinsville, Mass. for the marriage of Charlie and Alice.

However there was to be cause for mourning before the year was out. In the fall of 1899, Frank suffered the loss of her sister Daisy Carlock Pollitt. Daisy (Anna Mirenda) Hubbard was Frank's younger sister, a graduate, like all the Hubbard girls, of Illinois State Normal University, Normal, Illinois. She and her husband, Alvin Carlock, lived in Berea, Kentucky, with their two sons, Frank and George, and were associated with the college there. After the death of Alvin Carlock in 1891, Daisy had remarried in 1895. Frank visited Daisy in Kentucky in April of that year, perhaps to attend her sister's wedding, and the photographs that she took show a rural world quite different from the urban setting she had become accustomed to. One picture shows Frank about to descend from a quaint old carriage with the assistance of a gentleman in a frock coat. The picture bears the inscription in Frank's hand, "'Lady Frances' alighting through the carriage door April 1895, Ky." Like a true Hubbard, she could relish playing the role of the grande dame, and be amused by her own pretension at the same time.

Daisy's second husband, the Rev. Flor Silin Pollitt, was a prominent Methodist elder. Frank had been delighted by the announcement that Daisy and the Rev. Pollitt were expecting a second child in the fall of 1899. The sisters were close. Frank and John had sent money to Hudson for the purchase of Daisy's graduation gown in March of 1879.[20] Daisy was a talented poet, and the two poems that she had written at the time of Edith's death were a great comfort to Frank. John had had them printed up in a commemorative folder and distributed to family and friends. Frank was devoted to the Carlock boys and would always be fondly supportive of Frank and George. Indeed, Frank Carlock (Daisy's oldest child) had been living with the Larkins in Buffalo and attending school with Harry for the past year. Fortune seemed to be smiling on the Pollitts. Flor had been made Presiding Elder of the district, and the couple had moved into Diamond Point, a stately mansion in Harrodsburg, Kentucky, that would have delighted Frank. The news that Daisy had died when the child was born in late October or early November must have come as a severe blow to Frank and cast a pall over the festivities in Whitinsville.

The marriage of Charles Hubbard Larkin and Mary Alice Whitin took place at noon in the Railroad Avenue home of Alice's widowed mother, Mrs Julia F. Whitin, of Whitinsville. Music was supplied by members of the Boston Symphony Orchestra, and the ceremony was performed under an arch of ferns and evergreen decorated with pink and white roses by two Episcopal clergymen of Worcester and Whitinsville. Little Ruth Larkin lead the wedding procession as flower girl, followed by Frances Esty, matron of honor, the groom and his best man, his brother Jack (John, Jr.). Harry and Harold Esty were among the ushers. Alice's sister, Betsy, was maid of honor, and the bride was given away by her brother, Frederick B. Whitin of North Uxbridge. The bride's white satin gown was decorated with orange blossoms and a pearl and diamond pin given her by the groom. The ladies were all elegantly attired, and it is interesting to note that Frank chose a black velvet gown trimmed with point lace and diamonds, undoubtedly in mourning for Daisy. Altogether it was a very elegant affair, and the pall of Uncle Albert Whitin's disapproval of the marriage of his favorite niece to a man who was neither a member of civilized Boston society nor of European origin seems not to have spoiled the festivities.[21]

As the century drew to a close, John and Frank found themselves comfortably and happily settled in a congenial world. The business was prospering beyond John's fondest dreams, the children were turning out quite satisfactorily, and Frank had established herself as a leader in social and intellectual circles in Buffalo. If there were storm clouds on the horizon, they were unaware of them as the family gathered to usher in the new century at 125 Hodge Avenue.

---

[1] Darwin D. Martin *The First to Make a Card Ledger: Story of the Larkin Card Indexes*, Buffalo, N.Y.,1932.

[2] BECHS, Larkin Company, Inc. Records, Bound Vol. 1.

[3] Ibid.

[4] It is interesting to note that as early as 1897 the management was reconsidering this public sale of stock. On October 3, 1897, Martin writes that he is "negotiating with Mr. Larkin for equal right in repurchasing from customer-stockholders stock of the Larkin Soap Mfg. Co. which J.D.L.& Co., and Mr. Hubbard alone, had distributed and which resulted ultimately in my ownership of Larkin stock to ten percent of the total." Martin *Autobiography*, SUNY Archives, p.191.

[5] DDM to JDL, MS letter, BECHS Larkin Company, Inc. Records.

[6] This was suggested to me in conversation by Evelyn Heath Jacobsen.

[7] BECHS, Larkin Soap Mfg. Co. Minutes, p. 34.

[8] Frank's first travel diary is dated June 23, 1897, and inscribed "Log Book and Little Journeys—Frances H. Larkin." I am assuming that this was not the first trip for John, though it may have been.

[9] The fact of John's acquaintance with the Hardings suggests to me that he had located them on an earlier trip to England, and this may account for Nellie's travelling with Frances and Bessie Kellogg.

[10] FHL *Travel Diary* 1897, London, Thursday July 23. Diary in author's collection.

[11] FHL Travel Scrapbook, 1897–1899 in author's collection.

[12] This was reported to me by my father, Harry H. Larkin.

[13] Several of these bills remain in the possession of his descendants.

[14] Reyner Banham, et al. *Buffalo Architecture: A Guide*, Cambridge, MA: The MIT Press, 1981, p.81.

[15] The Ellicott Club of Buffalo, Members Handbooks 1897, 1898, 1902, 1904, in BECHS Vertical File.

[16] FHL manuscript in author's collection.

[17] *Buffalo Evening Times*, June 8 1899, p. 3.

[18] Ibid.

[19] Ibid.

[20] JDL, Account sheets, BECHS Larkin Company Inc. Records loose in Bound. Vol. #3.

[21] Information on Alice Larkin's difficulties with her Uncle Albert I have from her daughter-in-law Mrs. Charles H. Larkin Jr., who told me that her uncle cut her off from her inheritance. Her uncle had taken Alice to Europe in the hope that she would ally herself with the artistic and aristocratic circles he loved, and he could not countenance her marriage to a man from the west and the son of a soap manufacturer. Details of the Larkin-Whitin wedding taken from unidentified clipping in FHL scrapbook.

John D. Larkin, age
17, July 2, 1863.

Mary Larkin Hoag (c.)
with her stepdaugh-
ters, Emma (l.) and
Sarah Hoag (r.), c.
1865.

John D. Larkin, 1874.

Hannah Frances Hubbard
at the time of her mar-
riage to John D. Larkin,
1874.

Dr. Silas Hubbard, 1876.
Father of Frances Hubbard Larkin.

Juliana Frances Read Hubbard, c.
1875. Wife of Dr. Silas Hubbard.

Darwin D. Martin, the boy
John D. Larkin hired as a
clerk in 1879. Martin rose
to become Secretary of the
company after Elbert Hub-
bard left in 1893. (Courtesy of
SUNY at Buffalo Archives)

Elbert G. Hubbard and Bertha
Crawford Hubbard, c. 1881.

John D. Larkin, c. 1880, and Edith May Larkin, shortly before her death at Idlewood in 1885.

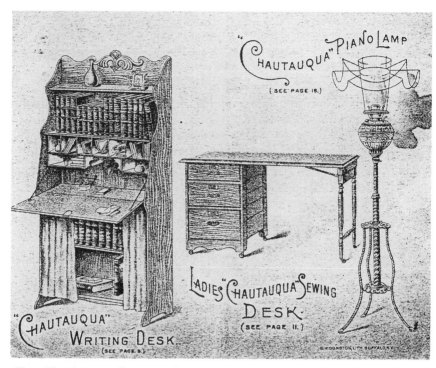

Top: The three earliest premiums of the Chautauqua line as shown on the back cover of the Premium and Larkin Plan circular entitled *Can We Break The Crust?*, probably issued in 1895. (Courtesy of Jerome P. Puma) Bottom: The Larkin Soap Mfg. Co., factory at 663 Seneca St., Buffalo, N.Y., 1895

Croquet on the Vicarage lawn, Barrow-in-Furness, Lancashire, England, 1897. Left to right: John D. Larkin, Mrs. Harding and John's cousin, Rev. Frederick Harding.

Tea at the Sharrott home in Surrey, England, July 1898. From left: Harry H. Larkin, John D. Larkin Jr., John D. Larkin, Ruth Read Larkin, Mr. Sharrott, unidentified child, Frances H. Larkin, Mrs. Sharrott (?), unidentified child, Frances Elberta Larkin, and Charles H. Larkin.

Chapter 7

Business and Family 1900-1910

For John and Frank the coming of the 20th century was filled with unlimited promise that New Year's Eve at 125 Hodge Avenue. Buffalo, a city which had burgeoned since 1875 into a thriving commercial center with a population of over 300,000, would host the world class Pan American Exposition the next year. Business leaders and city officials were already making preparations for the improvement of Delaware Park and the area to the north that would be the site of the great event. The Larkin Soap Manufacturing Co. had been reorganized under a simpler name—Larkin Soap Co., and on Seneca Street the "works" were expanding at a rate that must have delighted John with his passion for building. At home the two oldest children were newly married and already promising grandchildren. Charlie and John Jr. were at their father's side in the business, and Harry was on his way to a degree in chemistry at Lafayette College. Little Ruth, a lively and beautiful nine year old, filled the void left by Edith's death. Her parents doted on her, and she even attended the stockholders' meetings held at 125 Hodge Avenue where she helped count the ballots, and learned about business at an early age. Frank had found congenial friends in the intellectual and artistic circles of Buffalo, and, in spite of bouts of "the blues" that had plagued her since the days in Hudson,[1] was enjoying her role as a distinguished member of Buffalo society. With the troubles between Bert and Bertha settled satisfactorily, plans were being made for Dr. Silas and Mother Hubbard to move from Hudson, Illinois, to East Aurora to be near Bert and Frank. Altogether the arrival of 1900 must have seemed an occasion for rejoicing.

At the works, the orders had been coming in at a dizzying rate, and the problem of keeping up with demand was a serious one that put a strain on all concerned. Darwin Martin actually suffered a nervous breakdown in January of 1897, and John, with his usual concern for others, sent him off on an extended leave to recuperate.[2] After the struggles of the early 1890s, John was eager to translate the overwhelming success of the Larkin Soap Co. into his dream of a cooperative family of employers and employees working together in a safe and comfortable environment to bring premiums and products of the highest quality to the American home at the lowest possible cost to the consumer. He had known poverty and hardship as a boy; he felt keenly the value of a supportive extended family; and he wanted his to be a business that would reflect the values of the golden rule and enable the average family to flourish. In the 1880s the concept of the "Larkin Idea—Factory to Family" had been introduced. The middlemen eliminated by this approach had fought a losing battle trying to oppose the Larkin plan on legal grounds, and, when unsuccessful, many businesses tried imitation. Mildred Schlei points out that "most concerns deliberately copied Larkin ideas and imitated their premiums. After the year 1900, most of them disappeared from the field."[3] The quality service that the Larkin Soap Co. offered its customers and the comfortable, homey atmosphere that they fostered in their dealings with rural and small town families across the nation generated a business unequaled for its scope and for the devoted loyalty of its customers.

A matter of primary concern to John was the health and welfare of his employees. As the new buildings were built between 1895 and 1912, the first consideration was that they be fireproof, that light and fresh air be readily available, that mechanical efficiency and safety be of prime importance in all areas. He was fortunate in the men he had chosen to be his lieutenants. Darwin D. Martin and William R. Heath were men of principle, concerned, like John, with the integrity of the business, the welfare and comfort of the employees, and the general betterment of the human race. They believed in progress, and in the precept that success was the result of hard work, a respect for others and a determination to treat all men fairly. To a large extent they succeeded on the strength of these beliefs.

This concern for the welfare of the growing work force found expression in a number of innovations and improvements during the first years of the century. On May 1, 1900, the anniversary of the founding of the business, the hours of the factory help were reduced from nine hours forty minutes to nine hours without any reduction in pay. In the minutes of the stockholders meeting held at 125 Hodge Avenue on January 22, 1901, the Secretary's report mentions a number of "measures to more firmly unite the interests of employer and employee by making work pleasanter, easier and better paid."

The policy since 1897 of "erecting only fireproof structures with high ceilings and all interiors plastered and whitewashed has made surroundings more cheerful and healthful." In October of 1900, old "A" building was demolished, and the office was moved to roomier quarters on the 2nd floor of "E" and "F" buildings. The new building erected at the corner of Seneca and Larkin Streets (and still in use) was completed December 1, 1901, adding 200,304 square feet of floor and cellar space to the manufacturing capacity of the plant.[4] The minutes list a number of innovations in the new office space. A message carrier was installed "which places each of the more than 300 clerks practically at the elbow of all the others without expenditure of effort."[5] The new office space boasted a ventilating system "which replaces the entire atmosphere every three minutes," and prisms in the windows which diffused the daylight. Intercom telephones between all departments greatly improved their efficiency. A "comfortably furnished Rest Room (designed for the use of female help)," and a Coffee Kitchen that supplied coffee, cream and sugar free "to all female help" (at a cost of only $20.00 per week) was introduced. Vacations with pay "to old employees and the most meritorious" were inaugurated at this time, as well as an Employees Savings Department carrying 214 accounts at 5 percent interest.[6]

These improvements were only the beginning. In 1902 a piano was installed in the office area to provide recreation during the noon hour, and "to its strains the young women dance and sing as the mood seizes them."[7] A lunch room was opened in 1903 in a house at 680 Seneca Street where Frank Lloyd Wright's famous office building would rise in a few years. In the same year an employee publication was inaugurated entitled *Ourselves* which carried news and articles of interest to office and factory workers. Water filters were installed throughout the plant, and in that year the first employees' picnic was held. The Larkin YWCA was formed in 1905 and became an active organization with its women's Fife and Drum Corps and numerous activities. Men's organizations flourished as well, providing recreation and social opportunities for the men and boys. A plant library provided reading material, and eventually a branch of the Buffalo Public Library was opened. In 1907, the company established an Educational Department and offered to reimburse any Larkin employee attending school for all costs and expenses. The announcement concluded, "This Company would like to encourage any employee who has a real desire for self-imrovement and is willing to pay the price in effort."[8] A dental clinic was opened in the plant, as well as a fully staffed Doctor's office. The Company supported the YWCA in opening a dormitory and gymnasium on Seymour Street, and the Larkin Country Club, located on Lake Erie at Athol Springs, offered employees and their families accommodations during the summer season.

In the pages of the Pan American issue of the *Larkin Idea* Darwin D. Martin summed up the egalitarian philosophy of the Company as follows:

> *The Larkin Soap Co. is a harmonious unit in which many individuals have learned self effacement in earnest effort for the advancement of the common good. . . . The Larkin Soap Co. wisely concluded in the beginning that the new plan* [The Larkin Idea] *would not appeal so strongly to the dwellers in mansions, who leave to servants (who do not see, or feel concerned about, bills) to order by 'phone of the druggist, or from the grocer's handsome clerk on his daily rounds, the extravagantly advertised specialities of this and that soapmaker, whose methods . . . require a retail price three times the cost of the production; but safely reckoned upon the appreciation and loyal support of all who work and struggle, all who count cost — the millions, the salt of the earth.*[9]

These words are Martin's, but there is no doubt that they express the thinking and the character of John D. Larkin, whose relations with his employees were always man to man (or woman) and never boss to worker. One tangible result of John's attitude was the fact that none of the Larkin companies was ever threatened with a strike. In the same *Larkin Idea*, Martin tells of the visit to the Company of a representative of the New York State Labor Bureau, a Factory Inspector, who "pronounced the plant magnificent, and expressed great pleasure at the satisfied manner and appearance of the employees. 'If all working people were as considerately treated, there would never be need of strikes.'"[10]

An interesting slant on John's relations with labor is given in Darwin Martin's *Autobiography* wherein he relates an incident in the building of "D" building in 1896 to house the mammoth four story soap kettles:

> *Boiler makers were on strike in Buffalo in 1896. Quiet, always gentlemanly, Mr. Larkin was nevertheless pugnacious, and when the Union delegate assume* [sic] *to direct*

*Mr. Larkin to cancel the contract for kettles with Farrar &
Trefts he simply pointed out that this boiler-making firm had
the contract for the kettles and that they might proceed with
their contract if they could. They could. Work never stopped,
and the boiler-makers union for years proclaimed a national
boycott of the Larkin Co.[11]*

Characteristically, John refused to go back on his word and break a contract
that had been made in good faith.

As the plant expanded, the need for a power plant that could meet its
vast and diversified demands for steam and electricity became imperative.
In 1902, work was begun on the building that still stands at the southwest
corner of Seneca and Larkin Streets. This was to be a state of the art facility,
and the planning and building of the power plant must have been a source
of great satisfaction to the man who had struggled cutting timber in the
swamp in East Hamburg with the steam traction engine that he purchased
in 1868. The building was designed to accommodate twenty 500-horse-
power boilers fed by automatic stokers (eliminating hand firing and reducing the production of smoke to a minimum) using more than 100 tons of
coal per day. The stack that provided the draft for the fires and rose 250 feet
above Larkin Street was "by far the largest chimney in the city." The
factories were being equipped to be powered entirely by electricity, and the
new installation would provide an independent source of that relatively new
power, although it would be possible to connect to the Niagara Falls power
being distributed throughout the city if desired. The power plant would also
provide water under pressure to operate the vast sprinkler system as well as
compressed air for use as required.[12]

In 1903, Darwin Martin kept a detailed record of day to day business
at the works which sheds valuable light on John's involvement with the
business. It is clear that he was always in command of the ship, but always
in a quiet, unassuming way. John's attention to detail and deliberate approach to decision making had exasperated Darwin ten years before when
he wrote in his diary "Mr. Larkin is such a trifler and is so inclined to fritter
away with little details and to leave nothing to my authority he makes me
heartsick."[13] Not only Martin, but Will Heath and Will Coss often took
exception to John's views, but there was never any question where the last
word lay.

With regard to the power house chimney, there developed several
opposed points of view. Martin and Heath and other patrons of the Larkin
luncheon house signed an agreement that lettering be built into the brick

structure of the chimney. John was basically opposed to the idea, as were Will Coss, the factory superintendant, and John Jr.. Work was proceeding rapidly. When it was too late to add more than the word "Larkin," John reluctantly conceded that, if it could be done successfully, lettering should be added. At the same time he reminded Martin that it had been known "two weeks ago that no lettering was to be done." Martin reports that "Mr. Heath calls it 'star chamber' and says it isn't fair."[14] Cold weather halted work on the chimney for a short time; Martin reports opposition from Will Coss and John Jr.; and finally by February 23, John, after being told by Berrick, the contractor, that the chimney would crack if lettered, put an end to the whole argument. There would be no lettering.[15]

When the chimney was near completion, John Jr. happened to bring up at luncheon an account that he had read of a directors' dinner being held atop a similar chimney before it went into use. Martin had already thought of an identical plan, which he proposed, and all were in favor except Will Coss.[16] A few days later, when John was in New York, the question of the directors' dinner atop the chimney came up at luncheon, and Will Coss was asked by the group to see Mr. Berrick about the necessary carpentry. When John returned some days later, he and Will Coss went to the top of the chimney to survey the work, and when they came down, the workmen began tearing down the scaffold. Will Coss had never contacted Berrick at all. Harold Esty expressed surprise at luncheon that the plan had fallen through, and Will Coss said that he had left word for Berrick to call, but had received no reply. "Mr. L said 'It is just as well.'"[17]

Darwin Martin, of course, had seen the whole affair of the chimney dinner as a wonderful advertising stint, and he pointed out to John that "... we have twice paid $1,000 for less advertising than this would have given."[18] Will Coss, on the other hand, lacking the advertising man's passion for publicity, perhaps knew his employer better. By letting the whole matter slide, he undoubtedly carried out John's real wishes in the matter.

Jack Quinan, in his thoughtful and detailed study of the Larkin Administration Building designed by Frank Lloyd Wright, makes a keen observation on the tensions within the management of the Larkin company:

> *The Larkin clients—John Larkin, Darwin Martin, William Heath, William and Daniel Coss, and Mr. Larkin's two oldest sons, Charles and John, Jr.—represented a many-headed hydra of motives and opinions, stemming, in part, from a sharp division in the company between the soap-manufacturing and the mail-order businesses. Mr. Larkin, his sons,*

and the Coss brothers tended to identify themselves with the basic production of soap and related products, whereas Darwin Martin appears to have been principally responsible for the growing success of the accessory mail order business. William Coss was openly hostile to Martin on many issues, and John Larkin, Jr., who would eventually assume control of the Larkin Company and force Martin to resign, was also antagonistic. [19]

That John was more interested in one part of the business than another, I would question. His vision, I believe, encompassed the whole. However, having surrounded himself with capable men, he was wise enough to remain aloof from their differences and to rely on their best judgment. If need be, he was quite capable of quietly vetoing any proposal that he might see as detrimental to the best interests of the Company, and they all recognized his word as final. At the same time, he would abandon a pet project, if Martin or Heath could persuade him it was unwise. John kept constant pressure on his lieutenants to expand all facets of the business, manufacturing and mail-order, and was vitally concerned with its growth eventually, perhaps, to the point of overexpansion.[20] John loved to build, to see things grow and prosper, and he loved this growth for what it could do for those who worked to achieve it—family, employees, and customers.

In 1900, a great opportunity to promote the growth of the Larkin business lay just ahead with the Pan American Exposition. John had been fascinated by fairs and expositions all his life, and his company had already been represented in several such ventures before the Pan American. In April, 1898, the first Larkin exhibit was held in New York at the Industrial Health Exposition and Trained Nurses Educational Exhibit in the Grand Central Palace Industrial Building. That same year The Larkin Soap Mfgr. Co. was represented at the Omaha Exposition and was awarded the Gold Medal for Soap. Fully engaged as he was in the affairs of his rapidly expanding business, and in view of his desire to keep out of the limelight, it is not surprising that John's name does not appear among those of the directors and movers of the Pan American Exposition. John invested in the venture, purchasing ten shares in June of 1900, and he must have been vitally concerned with the planning and construction of the Larkin building that displayed the treasures his company offered the American housewife, but he left it to Darwin Martin to serve actively on one of the committees and to ride in the opening parade on May 1, 1901.

The story of the Pan American, its triumphs, its failures and its tragedy, has been amply told and documented, but little if anything has been said about the Larkin Soap Company Building. The official handbook of art and architecture of the Exposition lists: "THE LARKIN SOAP BUILDING. The main structure is classic in treatment, and is surmounted by a dome in the spirit of the Italian Renaissance, designed by Lansing & Beierl of Buffalo, New York."[21] The building was located on the east side of the grounds just across the canal from the Manufactures and Liberal Arts building and south of the Restaurant. One account claimed "an average daily attendance of 8,000 people."[22]

There was a large domed space at the center of the building "wherein is displayed a small working exhibit which gives a glimpse of the methods which are pursued in the manufacture of soap."[23] Only the finishing steps could be demonstrated in the space available: the milling process, the pressing and the wrapping of the finished bars. Each visitor was given a cake of soap as a souvenir. The central area under the dome was surrounded by columns, each apparently made up of one or another of the many Larkin products: cans of talcum powder, bars of Sweet Home soap, bottles of sachet or perfume, to name a few. In alcoves surrounding the central court displays were set up exhibiting the range of Larkin premiums available to the buyer of Larkin products. A Reception Room, a Library, a Music Room, a Dining Room, and a Bedroom, all completely furnished with items from the Larkin Premium Lists, showed the public what could be achieved with the purchase of Larkin products and premiums.[24]

In his letter to the company, Hugo Loeb remarks on the "homelike disposition the visitors manifested . . . as though they were calling at the home of some near friend."

> *Upon inquiry I was informed that the reason for this was the fact that the majority of the visitors were patrons of the house. Evidently their manner was an indication of satisfaction with the just and kindly treatment of the firm in all its dealings. In all my travels I have never seen such a manifestation of interest by a visiting public, as a compliment to a business with whom they sustained relations of trade.[25]*

John was never a man to let an opportunity to sell his soap go by. The man who sent Combination Boxes and Chautauqua desks to Col. Verbeck, Dr. Blakeslee, and practically everyone he corresponded with, had another ace up his sleeve. Why not bring the interested public into the factory and let them see the soap making process first hand? Visitors to the Exposition

118

were invited to visit the "works" at Seneca, Larkin and Carroll Streets, and they came by the hundreds. The *Buffalo Courier*, referring to the magnitude of the plant, called it "one of the wonders of the city."[26]

> *Uniformed guides, appointed solely for the entertainment of the visitors, take the sightseers in hand and lead them step by step through the great plant. . . Everything about the building is as clean and wholesome as modern science can make it. . . everything is placed under the closest scrutiny and its purity is instantly apparent.[27]*

The article continues with a discussion of the excellent relations maintained between management and labor, pointing out the care taken by the former to provide optimum conditions for every member of the Larkin business family. The memory of the Pan American will fade, but the Larkin Idea will continue to bring "lasting benefit to the city of Buffalo itself."

The Pan American ran its course through the summer of 1901. Frances Esty served as an usher at a concert in the Temple of Music on Flag Day. Frank and Alice took out-of-town guests to the affair, where they heard patriotic speeches by military and religious leaders, enjoyed the stimulating strains of Sousa's Band and attended a tea in the Women's Building.[28] The Larkins visited the grounds on several occasions, and Frank notes in her diary the impressive sight of the electric lights that outlined the buildings and the great tower at night.[29]

On that fateful 6th of September when President McKinley was shot, John and Frank were in New York staying at the Waldorf Astoria. Frank records in her diary how shocked they all were at the dreadful news. The Larkins returned to Buffalo the next day and went right to their home in Canada, but Frank's diary details the day by day reports on McKinley's progress. On Friday, September 13, she writes: "A Dark Friday—The President has collapsed. One of the papers says a flock of black birds flew over the Milburn house early this morning." The next day Frank reported that "The President died at two fifteen this morning, and lies only three blocks from our home in Buffalo." She adds that "Mr. Larkin went into Buffalo as soon as he heard the sad news."[30]

The events following the death of the President are detailed in a letter that Frank wrote to Harry at Lafayette College:

> *Well, what a sad, sad time we have had since you went away a week ago. . . It has made us all sick. Do you know I*

thought perhaps you would come home to see the procession.
John [Jr.] stood in line for two hours and then was so tired
and faint that he gave it up—but Uncle Will [Heath] and the
Coss boys had no difficulty. But it is better that you remember
him as he was, for they said he looked thin, drawn and as
though he had suffered. Papa was on Delaware Ave when
"Teddy" came the second time. He said he had his hat off
and was leaning forward and looking down—and looked
sad—pale—and troubled. There was a guard of mounted
police around the carriage. . . Frances said that there are so
many people around the Milburn House today that they still
have to keep two policemen there. While the [funeral] pro-
cession passed, each church they passed tolled the bells. St.
Paul's chimes played Nearer My God to Thee![31]

So the Pan American drew to a close under the pall of the assassination. Interestingly there is no mention of the Larkin building at the Pan American in Frank's diary, and indeed little mention of the business at all. Her life had become increasingly distanced from the concerns on Seneca Street with the move to Hodge Avenue, and by 1901 John's world of business probably seemed pretty remote and dull. In addition, for both John and Frank, events occurred in the two opening years of the century which channeled their interest and enthusiasm in new directions. In September of 1900, John purchased from Mr. Rumsey an estate on the Canadian side of the Niagara River at Queenston, and a year later in November of 1901, he purchased from Mr. Frank H. Goodyear a large house and property at 237 North Street. The first would open up to John the realization of his dream to establish a farm that would, unlike the East Hamburg venture, be a success. The house on North Street would provide a more suitable residence for the successful business man.

John had always had a soft spot in his heart for Canada, his mother's home, where he had spent many happy times as a boy and young man. He and Frank were both attracted to the Niagara-on-the-Lake area where they had visited their friends the Jacksons. In 1899, the last barrier to easy access to Canada was removed with the building of the suspension bridge at Lewiston, and John was ready to consider the move. An attempt to acquire property at Niagara-on-the-Lake had fallen through, when on the 15th of August, 1900, the real estate agent, Mr. Atwater, telephoned John to inform him that the Rumsey place at Queenston, Ontario, was for sale. Frank lost no time calling on her friend Mrs. Jackson who told her that "there was an old Colonial house on the 'Rumsey place,' that the roof leaked dreadfully and everything was out of repair. That there were two big fireplaces—and that it could be fixed up beautifully if one could go to the expense."[32] The following Saturday, John and his son Harry went "with Mr. Atwater to Lewiston and rowed across the river and climbed the *earth* steps to see the place Glencairn." John knew at once that it was what he and Frank had dreamed of and that he was in a position to make it theirs. He made a cash offer to Mr. Rumsey which was refused.

The following week Frank was packed and ready to go at a moment's notice to Glencairn, but John could not get away from the works until the end of the week.

> *Saturday, Aug. 25—We took the train at the Terrace, changed at Niagara Falls, took the Gorge Car and went to Lewiston. While waiting there for the ferry we could see the country house through the trees on the Canadian bank of the river.*[33]

Mr. Rumsey's caretaker took them through the house and grounds and Frank records:

> *The place far exceeds my expectations. The trees are beautiful.*[34]

John made a second offer which Mr. Rumsey accepted, but there followed ten days of delay because some of the papers could not be found. Finally on the 7th of September, John was able to telephone Frank from the office that the papers had been found and that Glencairn was to be theirs. There were some further delays. On the 9th of September they took their first company down to Glencairn—Mr. Heckman,[35] Edna Crate, John Jr., Harry and Ruth. "We took our white fantail pigeons in a basket—a fine luncheon under the trees and looked our new old house over thoroughly. We liked it all more than ever."[36]

Finally all the papers were completed, the deal was concluded and by the middle of September they were able to take possession of "Glencairn Hall." Frank writes, "Edna came down with Ruth, Mary the maid, John Jr. and Bobbette the Angora cat. Mr. Larkin and I came down on the Michigan Central train at 4:30 P.M.. That was our first night here—John and Edna were rowed over and went to Buffalo last night. The next morning cool & damp, no cream for our coffee. Sent Frank [a gardener] to Clifton for a new stove—made a kitchen upstairs—basement too damp and musty. We all worked hard to have things nice when Mr. L. and the Estys came. They are all delighted."[37]

The weeks that followed were filled with the pleasure and excitement of settling in. Glencairn Hall had been built in the 1830s, on the site of a War of 1812 battery, by one of the Hamilton brothers, shipbuilders at Queenston whose family gave its name to the city of Hamilton, Ontario. The house stood looking east over the Niagara River surrounded by stately trees and woods. It was built in classic Colonial style with a small porch on the driveway side and a double porch across the front on the river side. The kitchen and a small dining room were in the basement. Entering from the drive, one came into a central hall that ran through to the great porch. To the left off this hall, on the north side of the house, a large living room with two fireplaces ran from front to back. To the right off the hall was a reception room with another fireplace, and a large walk-in closet. Beyond the reception room a small hall went off to the right. From this hall a door to the right led into the reception room, and another to the left opened into a room which served for formal dining with two windows facing onto the veranda, a fireplace and a dumb waiter. From the main hall, a sweeping staircase led up to the second floor and the hall ended in several steps that led down to the door opening out onto the veranda on the river side of the house. To the left on the second floor the master bedroom, which had originally been used as an upstairs parlor, faced the river. French doors opened onto the upper veranda and there was a fireplace, a window facing north beside the fireplace, and a large closet. The bedroom in the north west corner of the house, with two windows looking over the drive and one looking north, also had a fireplace, but no closet. The sewing room occupied the space between the two west bedrooms, looking out over the drive, and the fourth small bedroom in the south east corner had two windows looking across the veranda to the river. Over the next few years the Larkins added bathrooms in the old part of the house and a wing to provide for a dining room, pantry and kitchen on the first floor and for an additional bedroom and bath as well as maids' rooms and baths on the second floor. The grounds, or "park" as Frank referred to them, had been neglected and work was begun almost at once establishing a garden.

The garden would provide Frank over the years with an ideal outlet for her love of beauty and sense of the dramatic. She had fallen in love with the gardens at Castle Hale and the other homes of friends that she had visited in England, and here was an opportunity to have such a place of her own. Within a few years she had developed a fine English garden complete with a dovecote of her own design.

In another vein, her garden would give expression to Frank's share in the current fascination with Japanese art and customs. In June of 1905, she and Mr. Calvert (John's farm manager) measured for a Japanese tea house and garden. By September her dream was realized, tea house and garden were complete, and Charlie photographed his mother in full Japanese dress standing by the steps admiring a lily. In October, Frank Lloyd Wright and his wife, just back from Japan, came to Glencairn, and the architect pronounced the tea house and garden a great success much to Frank's delight.[38] In 1905, Blanche Elizabeth Wade, the daughter of a friend, published a book, *A Garden In Pink*, which not only was inspired by the garden at Glencairn, but was illustrated with photographs of various views of the garden and park. The book, issued at Christmas, was given a full window display by the publisher, A. C. McClurg of Chicago, and became a best seller.

In further pursuit of her literary interests, and sharing her son Harry's love for the writings of the naturalist, John Burroughs, in 1903 Frank encouraged the building of a cabin in the woods north of the house. Harry and his cousin Ralph Hubbard, together with brother Charlie, cherished this rustic retreat, named "Slabsides" after Burrough's home on the Hudson. In her *Glencairn Log* Frank writes:

> *Yesterday I talked with the man who is hewing the logs for Harry's cabin. With his ax and his broad-ax he makes a fine piece of work of it. The hewing of logs is almost a lost art since timbers are sawed. The logs he hews are almost as smooth as if planed.*[39]

The first days at Glencairn in 1900 were filled with activity and excitement. The autumn weather was perfect. The first Saturday, Mr. Jackson "drove in with his brake and four-in-hand and took Ruth to St. Catherines."[40] John and Frank bought a horse—"Billie"—and "a sort of buckboard cart." Mrs. Jackson and a friend were the first formal visitors and there was a constant coming and going of family and friends. They walked in the "park," gathered wild asters and goldenrod, and competed to identify the birds that darted among the branches overhead. There were blazing fires in the drawingroom when the travellers came in from the train at Queenston or climbed the bank from the row-boat that brought them over from Lewiston. Everyone helped to gather stones for a new cairn to be erected near the house that would be larger than the one at the gate that gave the place its name. Will and Mary Heath came, and Mary enjoyed rowing over in the boat to meet the men returning from the "works." Bertha Hubbard and her sister Miss Crawford came on the 6th of October, and on that day Frank recorded, "Great excitement at Glencairn Hall. A telephone message sent to Mr. Jackson at Riverscourt that Frances has a little daughter born at 9:45 A.M. We are almost prostrated with the news that we are grandparents."[41]

In the first weeks, they discovered a wine cellar under the carriage house, watercress in the ravine, and an old bake oven. Their first chickens— barred Plymouth Rocks—arrived on October 26, much to Frank's delight. On the 27th, Dr. Silas and Juliana Hubbard, who had recently moved to East Aurora, came to see their daughter's new home, bringing narcissus bulbs from the old homestead in Hudson, Illinois. "Father climbs the bank-walks and roams about. Mother went to Niagara-on-the-Lake. The woods, park and everything beautiful. We are packing to go back to Buffalo."[42] Later the family returned to taste December in the country, but would not come back to stay until the following April.

Glencairn became a summer retreat for almost the whole family. John and Frank built homes for Charlie, Harry and Frances on land south of the main property along the river road toward Queenston.[43] The family of John Jr.'s fiancee, Edna Crate, had a home on the south shore of Lake Erie, and, after they were married in December 1900, John and Edna always spent their summers there. However, there was constant travel back and forth between Queenston, Buffalo and the U. S. lake shore. The Kelloggs had an elegant estate, "Lochevan," on Lake Erie at Derby, and, although with the advent of the automobile travel time was greatly reduced, it was still a long haul. There are wonderful pictures in the old photo albums of Larkins and Kelloggs seated high in the latest model Franklin, the ladies in their dusters and great veiled hats, the men in their vizored caps seated staunchly at the wheel or struggling with the not uncommon tire change.

The idyllic life on the river would continue until World War I. Frank's Log ends with an August entry in 1915. Except for Harry who shared his father's passion for farming, the others in the family felt remote from business and friends living in Queenston. The urge to join John Jr. and the Kelloggs on Lake Erie was strong. Frances and Harold Esty were the first to move. Harold, who was keenly interested in horses and riding, purchased a farm in Derby, NY in 1913, and then property on the lake where they built a summer residence. John Jr. was already interested in property at Sturgeon Point, a little farther west on the lake shore, which he acquired at about the same time. In 1916, Charlie, devoted to the simple life in the manner of John Burroughs, bought property in the wooded hills of Eden, NY. Over the years he added considerably to his original land, and today the property is set aside as a county park. Harry was the last to move, in 1916, purchasing a place on the lake between the Estys and the Kelloggs which he and Ruth named "Skylands." In spite of this move, Harry remained attached to the farms in Canada, which he continued to manage long after his father's death.

At Glencairn, Frank was more at peace with herself, less subject to "the blues," and the house and garden provided her with some of the happiest days of her life. John, too, found Glencairn a perfect retreat from the demands of business, and his farms were a source of deep satisfaction over the years. However, after the outbreak of the war and Bert's death in 1915, Frank found the Canadian experience increasingly difficult. In May, 1915, John cooperated with the Canadian military by making Glencairn available as a border guard post. Soldiers were stationed on the property to keep watch for espionage activity along the river. Frank wrote in the last pages of her Glencairn Log :

> *It seems two German spies have been caught—one here enlisted in the Canadian Army—and one at Windsor opposite Detroit. There has been a dynamite plot unearthed, and dynamite has been found smuggled over the border in suit cases in private motors. Tonight, 27th of June [1915]—as we entered our grounds we met two soldiers—another bringing hot coffee here on the road. A tent at the head of our stairs to the river and five men on duty. At the last landing near the river one of the soldiers told Mr. Larkin that he had been three years in the Boer War. That there were heliograph signals on the river banks here. That they were unable to read them. An American Government boat is patroling the bank on the American side tonight. And this is a part of the war between Germany, England, France, Belgium, Russia and Italy, and Elbert lost his life in this war! For over a year they have been fighting and still go on like beasts and animals. And we live in a so called Christian age![44]*

In the light of these events, it is not surprising that Frank found that she could not continue to live at Glencairn She purchased property in East

Aurora, and with Sanford Hubbard's help maintained a small farm there adjacent to the home her sister Mary and Will Heath had built. In an undated letter to John of that period urging the purchase of additional property, she states emphatically that "it is out of the question for me to go to Canada to live."[45]

John had acquired the Canadian farms over a period of time starting in June of 1901.[46] As we have seen, he had never forgotten his struggles managing his stepfather's farm in East Hamburg, but, at the same time, John loved the land, the animals, and the crops. He had fond memories of the Durrant farm at Winterbourne, Ontario, and felt a real kinship with the men who, like his grandfather Durrant, worked the land and provided the basic necessities for mankind. Now he had the business knowledge and the capital to operate a farm on a paying basis. When the Lewiston-Queenston bridge was built in 1899 and land on the Canadian side was available at bargain rates and easily accessible, John knew what he wanted to do. He first acquired the Rumsey place, Glencairn, as a home and then set about buying up farm land. Within a few years, John had established the Larkin Farms, which consisted of 1,900 acres of rich farm land. Nine hundred acres were on the escarpment south of Brock's monument, land now occupied by the giant reservoir that supplies the power plant on the Canadian side of the river. The remaining thousand acres were divided among several farms that stretched below the escarpment from just north of Glencairn towardNia-gara-on-the-Lake.[47] The earliest record of John's farming activity is a contract dated August 29, 1902, signed by John D. Larkin, agreeing to sell to E.J. McIntyre and G. N. Bernard of Niagara Township his entire crop of apples, except windfalls and twenty barrels of choice apples reserved for his own use, for $750 @ $1.00 per barrel. Any excess beyond the estimated 750 barrels to be paid for at the same rate.[48]

John's approach to farming was like his approach to manufacturing: managers chosen for their knowledge and integrity, efficient business methods, and concern for the well being of his employees were the principles on which he built. The Hill Farm on the escarpment was under the able management of Mr. James A. Calvert, and the farms along the river were directed by Mr. Allan A. Ramsey. The farms were divided into distinct departments such as sheep, cattle, hogs, fruit, general farm, day labor, each under a manager responsible to the general manager. Careful records were kept of all aspects of the daily operations of the farms, which made it possible to determine what procedures brought results. *The Farmer's Magazine* reported in 1917:

Each department manager reports daily at 6:30 a.m. to the manager so that he knows exactly where each of the 40 men employed is working for the day. Accurate recording of all details properly posted gives a very clear idea of department and job costs so that crop costs can be determined as nearly as possible. If there is a profit, the crop that brought it is known. Where losses occur, that is known to a certainty also.[49]

John's aim was always to build a plant that would be at once permanent, efficient and safe. At the same time, the plant must provide a comfortable, healthful and satisfying work place. Mr. Calvert shared John's love of building, and together they built splendid barns and farm buildings. *The Farmer's Magazine* describes the Hill Farm buildings:

On the Hill Farm entering beside the manager's house one would at a glance see that the principal farm buildings are arranged to form an immense courtyard all in view of the manager's house. The whole probably occupies about 20 acres. Arranged around this court and in following order are the Jersey barn, horse barn, implement shed, including blacksmith shop, 18 sheds and store room for tractor, as well as store room for large separator with, on the second floor, carpenter shop, paint shop and granary, then the piggery and finally the sheep fold. Each of these buildings would look very large on most farms and were substantially built of reinforced concrete by the present manager, Mr. Calvert.[50]

In addition to the impressive farm buildings, John and Mr. Calvert provided housing for the men with families on both farms. The houses were built on a common plan, thirty-five by thirty-eight feet square with three bedrooms, three clothes presses, dining room, kitchen and living room, front and back porch, a full cellar with a two barrel cistern, and each house had its own garden plot. Several of these houses are still to be seen on the River Road below Glencaim.

The farm equipment was always the latest and the best, from the great Rumley steam tractor to the common farm tools. With the best in living conditions and equipment, the Larkin Farms achieved a large and distinguished output. Marshall shows a picture of the Rumley hauling 1,000 bushels of wheat on seven wagons to the Shredded Wheat plant in Niagara

Falls. Everything was on a similarly large scale: twelve thousand apple trees, four thousand peach trees, ten thousand bushels of wheat and oats, twenty five to thirty tons of ensilage to the acre. "With a siding right on the farm shipping and loading facilities are the very best."[51]

John was particularly interested in livestock. He made trips to England to acquire the finest pedigreed pigs, Jersey and Aberdeen Angus cattle, Dorset and Southdown sheep. These animals were on several occasions accompanied by the farmers who had cared for them in England and who moved to Canada to work for John. The Larkin Farms became famous among livestock breeders as well as fruit growers, and over the years collected a vast array of ribbons and trophies at agricultural shows in Canada and the United States. These proofs of excellence were proudly and colorfully displayed in the barn offices and lined the walls of John's own study at home. John was never happier than when he put on his Wellingtons and went out with Mr. Calvert to lay out another barn, check on the offspring of the latest prize bull, or tramp through an orchard to see the ripening fruit that would win blue ribbons at the Royal Winter Fair in Toronto.

John had bought Glencairn in the fall of 1900; a year later, shortly after the assassination of McKinley and the inauguration of Theodore Roosevelt, he purchased 237 North Street from Mr. Frank Goodyear. The house was Victorian Gothic in style, of brick and stone with steep gables and a tower. Frank disliked it from the start:

> *Sat., Nov. 2, 1901—I drove on North St. with Frances and Miss Heckman to see Mr. Goodyear's place. A beautiful grounds with a little log cabin and trees, but such a monstrosity of a house! What would I do if I had to live under that tower, and those chimneys, and the coxcomb on the roof?*

> *Sun, Nov.3—We drove in the morning and went on North St to look at some houses. What crazy roofs, chimneys and towers some people have. Neither Elizabethan, Victorian, Colonial or Queen Anne!*

> *Monday, Nov 4 . . . I have told Papa that I will take the house if he will have the tower and chimneys taken off and the roof readjusted.*

*Tuesday Nov. 5 Mr. Larkin bought 237 North Street. I went
early and looked through. Mr. and Mrs. Goodyear were very
kind. I left Papa there and he telephoned me later that he
had bought the place. The grounds are beautiful. Of course
we would build a different house, but it is sunny and homelike.*[52]

Clearly Frank knew when she was defeated, and accepted John's
decision with a good grace. John arranged to give the house on Hodge
Avenue to Harold and Frances Esty, and Frank, in spite of ill health, began
the difficult transition. On Monday, December 9, 1901, she writes:

*We began to move. Mrs. Kehr and Mrs. Chauncey here
early. Had one carriage for them with the pails, mops and
scrubbing brushes, and we went ahead in our own carriage.
Staid until noon and went back to 125 Hodge Ave. and to
bed. Had to have my dinner taken up.*[53]

The following day the move was completed, and it must have taken a
considerable toll. The diary ends at that date, and there is no record of the
first Christmas in the new house.

To borrow a phrase from Oscar Wilde's Lady Bracknell, the fall of
1901 was indeed "crowded with incident" for Frank and John. Frank's
feelings of depression and poor health may well have had their roots in
events which preceded the move to North Street. In September of 1901 came
the first indication that the truce that had held in East Aurora since 1895 had
been broken. Wayland Woodworth, a lawyer married to Alice Moore's
sister, had assumed responsibility for the collection of child support from
Bert for Alice's daughter, Miriam. Bert had fallen in arrears some $3,500,
and Woodworth filed a suit to collect for his sister-in-law.[54]

The story broke in the Buffalo papers, much to the chagrin of all
concerned, and Frank and her parents were deeply hurt.

*Friday, Sept. 27—Glencairn A bad, bad day! Elbert Hub-
bard exposed in the Express. Pa and Ma, George [Carlock]
here. We came down on the three o'clock train. Ma's grief is
pitiful. There is nothing to say. We will have to resort to the
Power of Silence. It is harder for her and Bertha than for
anyone else.*

Sat. Sept 28—A bright sunshiny day. I am trying to keep Ma up. Pa and George went to Niagara Falls, Brock's monument, and on both the American and Canadian sides. Then Pa came back at six o'clock and went swimming and he eighty years old. I've talked and talked to Ma until I'm tired out. No use to try "The Power of Silence" on her.

Tues. Oct. 1—I'm tired out soul and body and am a wreck physically, mentally and spiritually. To think that our good name should be dragged down like this.[55]

During the next months the situation worsened. Alice moved to Concord, Massachusetts, and Bert spent more and more time with her and even took young Bert to Concord with him to acquaint him with Alice and his little half sister, Miriam.[56] For Bertha it became obvious that a complete break was the only viable alternative for herself and her children. John and Frank gave her every support. Norris Morey, of the prestigious law firm of Morey and Bosley, was retained to represent her case, and a divorce suit was filed on December 8, 1902. News of the separation had appeared in the *Buffalo Courier* as early as Saturday, December 6th. On Sunday, the *Courier* ran an authorized interview with Fra Elbertus in which he stated that he would not contest the suit and "that his mother, father and children approved of his course and his conduct toward his wife."[57] In the front page headline article of the *Courier* on December 9th, the paper reported that this interview "greatly incensed" the relatives of Mrs. Hubbard, including Bert's own sisters, Frances Larkin and Mary Heath, and that they "denounce this statement as a brutal misrepresentation, and authorize the publication of a statement refuting the allegations made by Mr. Hubbard."[58]

Frank's diary details the events of the next few weeks and the Christmas and New Year celebrations at 237 North Street. Allowing for her tendency to dramatize, it is clear that Bert's conduct came as a severe blow to the family and cast a pall over the closing days of the year. The family gathered at 237 North Street for Christmas. Harry was home from college, Bertha and Katherine were there, and Mother Hubbard and George Carlock came at noon on the 24th. There was a tree in the library, and Ruth and Katherine hung their stockings in front of the fireplace. Frank reports they were awake at 4 o'clock Christmas morning. The clan gathered early— "twenty three in all. Grandpa and Sanford came after we had begun distributing the presents."[59] After the presents, the married children returned to their own homes. There were eleven for Christmas dinner and Bertha and the rest of the family all made the best of a sad situation. The last week of the year passed in relative quiet. Frank visited her married children, went downtown with Harry, entertained the Heath children, and Bertha, Katherine and Ralph were at 237 North one day. Katherine stayed with Frank while Bertha and Ralph went out to East Aurora. Harry's roommate from college, Billie Rush, came early on the bright sunny morning of the 31st, and George Carlock came in from East Aurora. Frank had a long talk with George, probably about his future as an artist, and George and his Uncle John were involved in a discussion that saw in the New Year. There was much to take Frank's mind off her troubles. However, at the conclusion of the diary she writes:

> *The last three months have been soul racking on account of Elbert Hubbard's [illegible] actions and doings. We suffer shame, humiliation and torture that he is our brother. . . I never knew him to damn and swear, but now that Ralph has told me that he curses swears and damns his mother and himself—Surely he is one of those whose "great wits to madness are allied—and often do their bounds divide" and there is method in his madness. After the new year I shall begin the Biography of a many sided man.'[60]*

For all her rage and disappointment, Frank could not quite cut herself off from her adored but erring brother. She might vow to have no more to do with him, but she could not quite make the break.[61] Toward the end of January, 1903, there was an exchange of telegrams between Bert and Frank in which Bert begs her to intercede with Mr. Morey to avoid any publicity in the court proceedings regarding the alimony and child support suit.[62] Frank was in New York, but did her best on Bert's behalf. Ultimately Bert conceded the question of Bertha's custody of Ralph and Katherine and agreed to leave the amount of alimony to the judgment of the court. The trial before Judge Kenefick lasted two days. Young Bert and Sanford were in court with their father, and Ralph was there with Bertha. Justice Kenefick reserved decision on the alimony and the final judgment was handed down October 11, 1903, granting divorce and a settlement in Bertha's behalf of $1500 a year and $500 for each of the children in her custody.

There is no record of John's reaction to the conduct of his brother-in-law. Unquestionably his sympathies lay with Bertha and the children, as did Frank's. John had had some bitter experiences with Bert in the past, and his own character and temperament would have made it difficult for him to understand the flamboyant egotism that fueled the career of Fra Elbertus. He would have faced the facts, made his peace with them and gotten on with the business of life. Frank, on the other hand, shared enough of Bert's romantic temperament and artistic ambition to empathize with his feelings, although she could never condone his actions. As a result she was torn apart emotionally by what happened in East Aurora.

The Hubbard scandal not only undermined Frank's emotional and physical health; it also created a crisis in her faith and in her relations with the Baptist church. She and John had moved from the Prospect Avenue Baptist Church when they built on Hodge Avenue. The Larkins maintained their close friendship with Rev. E. E. Chivers of Prospect Avenue, whose photograph appears in the Glencairn Log for 1905, but had begun attending the Delaware Avenue Baptist Church much nearer home. Their daughter Frances was baptized in that church in April of 1890.[63] However, Frank had begun during the 1890s to form ties with St. Paul's Episcopal Cathedral through family and friends and to attend services there. Young Frances left the Baptist church in 1897 to become an Episcopalian. She was confirmed at St. Paul's in 1898, and was married there to Harold M. Esty in 1899. Charlie's Alice was an Episcopalian, and her two boys were both baptized at St Paul's. Frank's little Ruth Read Larkin was baptized at St. Paul's in June of 1902.

Family tradition holds that sometime shortly after the Hubbard scandal broke in the Buffalo papers in December, 1902, Frank was visited by a delegation of elders from the Delaware Avenue Baptist Church and asked to formally disassociate herself from her brother or leave the congregation. She chose the latter course, and on March 29, 1903, she was confirmed in the Episcopal faith at St. Paul's. The visit from the elders may not have been all that drew Frank to St. Paul's. The aesthetic appeal of the more colorful Episcopal ritual would surely have played a part in her decision. The whole experience of Bert's divorce was a trauma from which Frank never really recovered, and in the years to come she would seek solace in Eastern mysticism, Theosophy and Spiritualism as well as the Episcopal church.

---

[1] JDL LCB p. 148. In a letter to Mary Weller written May 21,1891, John reports, "We are all pretty well except Frank. The Doctor says she is suffering from nervous prostration."

[2] Martin, *Autobiography*, p. 186. Martin speaks of Mr. Larkin's kindness in holding a directors' meeting at Martin's house, assuring him that his plans

for the company would be "carried out fully," and sending him off for an extended rest.

[3] Schlei, *The Larkin Company* p.21.

[4] BECHS, Larkin Soap Company, Minutes p. 22.

[5] Ibid.p. 19.

[6] Ibid. pp. 18-20.

[7] *Buffalo Courier*, May 29, 1904, p. 2.

[8] *Ourselves*, May 15, 1907.

[9] *The Larkin Idea*, May-November, 1901, pp. 51, 55.

[10] Ibid. pp. 47,48.

[11] Martin, *Autobiography*, p. 184.

[12] *The Larkin Idea*, June 1903, pp. 2-5.

[13] Martin, *Autobiography*, p. 162.

[14] Martin, *Business Diary*, February 4, 1903. SUNY Archives. "Star Chamber" is a reference to the British court of law that sat without a jury and was infamous for its severe and arbitrary rulings.

[15] Ibid., February 23, 1903.

[16] Ibid., April 3, 1903.

[17] Ibid., May 4, 1903.

[18] Ibid.

[19] Jack Quinan, *Frank Lloyd Wright's Larkin Building: Myth or Fact*, p .8.

[20] Martin, *Business Diary*, passim. John was constantly seeking ways to expand the Larkin business as evidenced in his repeated suggestions for new products and premiums, his proposal to sell industrial life insurance (which Martin warned against: JDL dropped), his establishment of the Buffalo Pottery and Buffalo Leather Goods and purchase of the Greenburg Glass Company, and his repeated insistance upon making every move to expand, often against Martin and Heath's advice. Martin's entries for 1/13, 2/9, 3/10, 4/15 in 1903 all refer to JDL's pushing for 50 percent to 60 percent growth.

[21] *Art Handbook: Official Handbook of Architecture and Sculpture and Art Catalogue to the Pan-American Exposition*, Buffalo, N.Y.: David Gray, 1901, p.45.

[22] Letter from Hugo D. Loeb to the Larkin Soap Company October 10, 1901. BECHS—MS in Martin Collection, Box 5.

[23] *Buffalo Courier*, October 6, 1901, p.2.

[24] Ibid.

[25] Loeb, Letter 10/10/1901

[26] *Buffalo Courier*, 10/6/1901, p.2.

[27] Ibid.

[28] Frances H. Larkin, *Glencairn Hall: Larkin Log*, 1900–1915. p.15. Hereinafter referred to as *Glencairn Log*.

[29] Frances H. Larkin, Diary, June 14, 1901.

[30] Ibid. September 13, 14 1901.

[31] FHL, MS letter, September 19, 1901, in author's collection.

[32] FHL, *Glencairn Log* p.1.

[33] Ibid. p. 2.

[34] Ibid.

[35] A college friend of Charlie who was employed at the company and who would succeed Will Coss as Superintendant of the plant in 1909.

[36] FHL, *Glencairn Log*, p.3.

[37] Ibid.

[38] Ibid. p. 63.

[39] Ibid. p. 52.

[40] Ibid. p. 4.

[41] Ibid. p. 5.

[42] Ibid. p. 6.

[43] Harry H. Larkin was married to Ruth Williams on September 5, 1906. Ruth was a grandniece of Washington Irving, and the couple named their home on the Niagara River "Sunnyside" after Irving's home on the Hudson River.

[44] Ibid. pp. 94-95.

[45] MS undated letter in the author's collection.

[46] FHL, *Glencairn Log*, p. 17.

[47] A.P. Marshall, "Larkin's Departmental Farms," *The Farmer's Magazine*, Toronto, Vol.11, No.2, December, 1917.

[48] It is interesting to note that in 1867, in East Hamburg, John received $2.00 per barrel for apples. Of course, he was selling only a few barrels then.

[49] Marshall, "Larkin's Departmental Farms." Included in the discussion of the Hill Farm, but equally applicable to the farms under Mr. Ramsey's direction.

[50] Ibid.

[51] Ibid.

[52] FHL Diary, November 5, 1901.

[53] FHL Diary, December 9, 1901.

[54] Charles F. Hamilton, *As Bees in Honey Drown: Elbert Hubbard and the Roycrofters*, New York: A.S. Barnes and Company, 1973. p. 170.

[55] FHL, Diary, 1901.

[56] Hamilton, p. 175.

[57] *Buffalo Courier*, Tuesday, December 9, 1902, p. 1. Frank pasted the clipping of this article into her diary at the entry for this date.

[58] Ibid.

[59] FHL Diary, December 25, 1902. Frank's count of twenty-three must include three servants, perhaps the coachman, the cook, and a maid.

[60] Ibid. Memoranda.

[61] Frank had written to Harry on October 9, 1901: "I am so tired of hearing of the Roycroft and the cranks and vileness there . . . I am done with Bert until he can drop all deceit, two sidedness and immorality." MS letter, DIL Collection.

[62] MS documents in author's collection.

[63] Delaware Avenue Baptist Church baptismal records.

Chapter 8

Architecture and Art 1900-1912

The explosive growth of the the Larkin Soap Company in the opening years of the century created an urgent need to expand the manufacturing plant. In February of 1900, the directors authorized John to purchase and contract for expansion "as he sees fit."[1] Between 1900 and 1907 virtually all of the great complex of buildings on Seneca Street was completed. The giant warehouse was added in 1912. A notebook kept by Will Coss details the real estate transactions that were required to purchase the property needed for the expansion. Residences on Seneca, Larkin and Carroll Streets were bought up. Some houses were moved to new locations, some were demolished, and the owners were glad to realize something on their property and move away from the growing industrial area.

By 1902 it was obvious that the administrative and mail order departments of the business had outgrown the quarters provided for them in "E" and "F" buildings. It was decided to build a separate administration building across Seneca Street from the factory in the area west of Sacred Heart Church where the Larkin Luncheon house stood at 680 Seneca Street. John wanted the construction of the new building to be in the hands of R. J. Reidpath, architectural engineer, whose work on the factory buildings he knew and trusted. All that was needed was to select an architect to create the design. At first John wanted to give the commission to the renowned Chicago firm of Adler and Sullivan. However Darwin Martin had fallen under the spell of Frank Lloyd Wright, the young architect who had split with Adler and Sullivan and gone on to create some radically different homes in Oak Park. Darwin's brother William was enthusiastic about Wright's work, and the brothers agreed that Wright was the man to design the new office building. William Heath joined Martin in his enthusiasm for Wright's work, and together they pressed their case. John was perfectly willing to consider Wright for the job, and in November of 1902 Wright came to Buffalo for an initial conference.[2]

Building was a passion with John, and here was a man with new ideas and the courage to put them into effect. For all his quiet conservatism, John was fascinated by new approaches to dealing with problems. Always he wanted the newest and the best, from the steam traction engine on the farm in East Hamburg to his early interest in Robbins and the printing telegraph and the innovations in his factories and his farms. However, unlike Darwin Martin and William Heath, who both commissioned Wright to design homes for them in the city, John's interest in the modern did not extend to domestic architecture. Wright makes pointed note of this in his *Autobiography*. "In architecture they [the Larkins] were still pallbearers for the remains of Thomas Jefferson and subsequently all built colonial houses for themselves in Buffalo."[3] When it came to building a home, John and Frank favored the traditional American Georgian style. In Glencairn they had found a house they loved. Frank kept scrapbooks filled with pictures of prominent American homes of the colonial period. She had lived under the Victorian towers of North Street, and she wanted a home suited to a member of the DAR and a descendant of that soldier of the Revolution, Daniel Hubbard. Within a few years, John would build that home for Frank at 107 Lincoln Parkway.

However, the world of business was another matter. In creating an administration building for his thriving enterprise, John was willing to try something new. As the plans progressed, he saw that what Wright proposed would combine all the features that he had sought for his employees in an outstanding modern building. The Larkin luncheon house and its neighbors were razed, and at 680 Seneca Street the massive brick and sandstone structure rose between 1904 and 1906. The Larkin Administration Building would become world famous, a pioneer work in the development of modern architecture, a building of which John was always justly proud.

Across Seneca Street construction continued to expand the factory, and, as we have seen, by 1907 the entire complex of Larkin factory buildings was complete, with the exception of the 1912 warehouse. Since the Pan American Exposition the public had been invited to tour the Larkin factories, and in 1906, between January 1st and September 15th, 22,805 visitors had taken the factory tours.[4] In the fall of 1906, the administrative and mail order offices moved into the new building, and the visitor to the Larkin plant was offered a unique experience.

Turning his back on the factory buildings that loomed over the street behind him, the visitor approached Wright's brick and sandstone building through the gate on Seneca Street. The massive piers of the main building rose skyward on his left with its sculptured globes and figures atop the lighter central piers. Directly ahead stood the Annex with its main entrance. The air would be heavy with the mixture of industrial odors fair and foul that hung over Seneca Street—coal smoke from the nearby railroad mingled with the heavy smell of boiling soap and the delightful odor of roasting coffee. On the broad sandstone steps beside the fountain with its sheet of pure water splashing into the reflecting pool, the visitor might stop to read the motto carved into the intaglio plaque set into the brick of the Annex stair tower. HONEST LABOR NEEDS NO MASTER SIMPLE JUSTICE NEEDS NO SLAVES. Another flight of broad steps brought him to the heavy plate glass doors through which he would come in to the annex lobby.

As the glass doors closed behind our visitor, the noise and smells of Seneca Street would vanish. He entered a world where the quiet hum of the office replaced the noise of the outside world. The air in the lobby was fresh and cool. The graceful curve of the reception desk rose white[5] above the marble-like floor, and palms and ferns softened the masonry. A turn to the left past the cashier department's bronze wickets would bring the visitor out to the central court and into a world flooded with light from the skylight seventy five feet above the floor. High up under the skylight at each end of the court conservatories filled with plants and palms brought the world of nature indoors to the twelve hundred clerks and executives of the company who spent their working days here.

The main floor under the skylight and each of the balconies were filled with the metal desks Wright designed especially for the building. Their magnesite tops and panels echoed the horizontal slabs that topped the banks of filing cabinets and defined the balconies of the floors above. Around the top of the court at the fifth floor level, the balcony fronts carried inscriptions: at each end of the court quotations from the Sermon on the Mount, and on the sides of the court fourteen sets of three inspirational words in each panel. These inscriptions and the geometric gilded design of the sculptured pier capitals glistened in the light from above. The overall impression of this vast, light-filled space was one of serenity in what in fact was a teeming hive of business activity.[6] The visitor might well feel an almost religious awe.

John was delighted to see his business family so well provided for. He had worked hard over his sixty one years, and the fruits of his labors far exceeded his fondest dreams. His own office at the south end of the court and adjacent to the the Cashier's office was one part of a space set aside for the executives. The President's Office was barely separated from the main floor by half partitions of brick and glass topped with horizontal slabs of magnesite. This semiprivate area consisted of a central space that looked out onto the main floor, flanked by two smaller spaces, John's office on the left and a directors' room on the right. There were no doors. The large plate glass windows above the cabinets along the outer wall filled the space with light here as throughout the building. John furnished his own office with his mahogony desk and chairs, a sofa, and metal file cabinets with a dark wood-grain finish along the wall beneath the window. He was more at home with these familiar furnishings than with Wright's tawny metal and magnesite.

Seated at his desk, John could look out to the central space where John Jr. and Charlie and Harry had their desks, and it was but a few steps to the Accounting office to keep his finger on the pulse of the business. Out in the central court, the two men whom he had come to rely on so heavily to manage the premium business and the office staff, William Heath and Darwin Martin, sat at open desks surrounded by the women and men who made the operation possible. The one was his brother-in-law, the other he had taken in as a boy. Looking up through the window to his left, John could see a part of the upper stories of "H" building and the large letters of the sign that ran around the top of the entire block of buildings announcing: LARKIN CO SOAPMAKERS REFINERS PERFUMERS CHEMISTS. Over there were the men who made the products: the soap, the perfume, the coffee, the peanut butter, the macaroni, the vanilla and spices and puddings. C. F. Booth, a brilliant chemist, dealt with the formulas. Will and Dan Coss saw to the manufacturing and shipping. John felt great affection for those men. Remembering his own struggles with Weller's soap kettles he felt close to the workers in the factory. He had done it all—the soapmaking, the slinging, the bookkeeping—and now he could feel assured that what had started when he left the farm in East Hamburg to join forces with Weller rested in the hands of a family of loyal workers and customers who shared his vision. At the heart of that vision was a very strong ideal of responsibility and service, an ideal that had its roots in the concept of the brotherhood of man. In 1899, John had written to Darwin Martin:

> *Our opportunities for doing good to our fellow men increase with the growth of our business and we must not do anything to reduce or limit the far reaching influences which we have in our power to extend.*[7]

A business was not just a means of making money, it was a trust, a tool for serving one's fellow human beings. John was a man for whom the Sermon on the Mount was a blueprint for life. Friends of Charlie and Alice from England who visited in 1907 summed up the view of John and his fellow administrators in a letter written on their return home: "I see with delight another great proof of the immense impulse toward better human relations which is a real working religion . . . That is the central point—that the stewardship of such power is so faithful and true."[8]

The Administration Building that Wright designed for the Larkin Company was a source of considerable pride to all members of the Larkin business family. Employees who worked in the building had only the highest praise for the beauty and serenity of their work place. Visitors came to Buffalo from all over the world to see the building and were filled with admiration. There were, however some problems with Wright's ideas. The metal furniture was extremely heavy, and the three-legged office chair so unstable it came to be known as the "suicide chair."[9] Over the years the building proved to be expensive to heat, and maintenance was a continuing problem. Perhaps the most serious problem arose in connection with the red sandstone that Wright chose for the exterior details of the building. The failure of this stone to resist the rigors of Buffalo winters resulted in 1915 in the death of a young telegraph operator. On Thursday, February 18, a large piece of an exterior ledge which had cracked on the fifth floor, somehow came loose, falling through the skylight of a first floor office on the Swan Street side and instantly killing 21 year old Jane M. Lannon at her desk.[10] John and the rest of the Larkinites were deeply shaken. The business had always prided itself on reducing industrial accidents to the very minimum. Employee safety had always been a first priority. After the accident the management took a hard look at the exterior of the building and determined to remove the sandstone sculptures that stood atop the piers at each end of the building.[11]

While John was dealing with the man who would come to be recognized as the greatest architect of the 20th century and guiding the growth of the business, Frank was tending to the home front and pursuing her interests in art, literature and the world of ideas. It was a time of change and growth in the family circle. There was the move from Hodge Avenue to North Street, there were marriages and the arrival of more grandchildren. In the spring of 1902, Frank records in her diary, "Grandma came in [from East Aurora] and we had the photograph of the four generations taken. Elberta would not sit on her great grandmother's lap and we were all most anxious for her while we were sitting."[12] The new home in Queenston and the farms there added a whole new dimension to the life of the family. These years were among the happiest that John and Frank spent together. In spite of his preoccupation with the demands of business, John always put his family at the top of his agenda, and he was always there for Frank and his children. He took a lively interest in the orchids that Frank delighted in growing on Hodge Avenue and in the greenhouse on the new property on North Street.

He sometimes attended the lectures that Frank and her friends held at their homes. A Dr. Willis lectured on "The Astral Light," on Emerson, and delivered a lecture on Christianity in the parlors at 125 Hodge Avenue. John's views on Frank's interest in spiritualism and the occult would be interesting, but one suspects that he probably quietly refrained from comment. John's quiet Christian faith would have had little need of the eccentric spiritism of Mme Blavatsky or Annie Besant.

Frank's social life was a busy one, with the usual obligations to call on friends, entertain at tea, and keep up with the activities of the DAR and other women's groups to which she belonged. For one of these groups the members were expected to prepare and present papers on subjects of historical and current events. One such paper that Frank prepared bears the title "Central Asia In the Past and Prospectively" and presents an informed discussion of the history of that region with emphasis on Russian expansion to the east in recent years. There were, too, the gala events which she and John attended together, such as the Charity Ball held New Year's night at Convention Hall and the DAR Colonial Tea and Ball held in January at the Twentieth Century Club. Of the latter Frank writes:

> *The Colonial Tea and Ball at the Twentieth Century Club.*
> *Busy there all day. Philip* [the Larkin's coachman] *went to*
> *sleep and did not come for us at one o'clock. We walked*
> *home in deep snow. Beautiful flowers, silver, laces, jewels.*
> *Last night's or this morning's walk home was a fitting ending*
> *for the Colonial Ball.*[13]

There is no suggestion of blame for Philip's defection. She and John must have felt that he deserved his rest, and were quite happy with the exhilerating walk through the snow to 237 North Street.

Early in 1902, two events occurred that greatly intensified Frank's already considerable interest in art. In January, Lars Sellstedt began work on a portrait of Frank. She was delighted to get to know the 83-year-old artist and his family. Sellstedt had made a considerable reputation for himself as a portrait painter and landscape artist. He was one of the founders of the Buffalo Fine Arts Academy, had travelled widely and published an autobiography detailing many of his adventures. Frank was fascinated that he had met Madame Blavatsky, the famous mystic and founder of the Theosophical movement, and "so many interesting people." His daughter, Mrs. Potter, had seen Robert Browning "several times on the streets of Rome but was not presented to him."[14] At this same time, George Carlock, sister Daisy's son, a youth of eighteen, came to East Aurora to visit his grandparents, Dr. Silas and Grandma Hubbard. He visited his Aunt Frank and Uncle John in early February and expressed his enthusiasm for a career in art, perhaps influenced in part by his Uncle Bert and what he had seen at the Roycroft. Daisy's loss had been a great blow to Frank, and her heart went out to the two Carlock boys who had lost both their father and their mother. Frank, the elder, had lived with the Larkins on Hodge Avenue and attended "Cap" Mellen's school with Harry in 1898. She and John determined to look after the schooling of the younger boy and help him with his ambition to be an artist. Arrangements were made for George to attend Mr. Wheeler's Heathcote School and a "life class." "Maybe he will be one of the coming XX Century artists."[15]

The story of George Carlock's career in art extends over the next two decades until his death in 1918. The boy lived with the Larkins on North Street while attending school and in the summer of 1902 he was at Glencaim. Frank's diary records that he was in East Aurora and came in with his grandparents to that sad Christmas when Bertha sought refuge at 237 North Street.[16] He came in to Buffalo on New Years Eve, and Frank records, "I've had a long talk with him. He and his Uncle John sat up until after the New Year and talked."[17] This would certainly suggest that serious plans were afoot for the boy's future.

There is no record of his activities in 1903, but, by the spring of 1904, George was writing to his grandmother and Aunt Frank from the National Arts Club in New York City. During the summer of 1904 he was studying at Lyme, Connecticut, and spending time sailing and painting at Hamburg, a village near Lyme.[18] There he rented a "studio" for $2.00 a month and hoped to do several large pictures for annual exhibitions in New York. In October he was at Glencaim and signed his name in Harry's "Slabsides" guestbook. Frank was in the process of cataloging her library, and she commissioned George to design a bookplate for her. There was a good deal of trial and error before he and his aunt finally settled on the design showing a Viking ship with King Hubba's raven emblazoned on its sail approaching land. The design was set in an ornate border above FRANCES HUBBARD LARKIN done in old English lettering. John undoubtedly had the final engraving, which was done on parchment paper, printed by the art department at the company. Frank must have been pleased, for she used the plate throughout her very extensive collection.

In January of 1905, George was in Howard Pyle's composition class at the Art Students League of New York on 57th Street. "I will try hard for another year as we said last spring and will study illustrating and composition in Mr. Pyle's Composition class and coppying [sic] landscapes at the museums and then if I cannot get enough to do I think I will go into some commercial branch." It is clear that his aunt and uncle hoped that he would soon be able to make his living with his art, perhaps as a portrait or landscape painter or even as a commercial artist. Little did they know that here was a chip off the old Hubbard block—a stubbornly dedicated soul whose vision of his own integrity as a man and an artist would tie him to ten more years of hard work and study.

George came to Buffalo from time to time. He did an undated sketch in Harry's cabin guest book again in 1905, and in January, 1906, one of his paintings from the summer at Hamburg, Connecticut, was exhibited at the Albright Art Gallery.[20] In March John and Frank had dinner with George at the Waldorf in New York.[21] They had attended a picture sale that day, and perhaps their meeting with George involved a discussion of his plans to go to Paris for further study. He must have left for France during the summer or fall and taken up his studies there with the continuing support of his aunt and uncle.

In the spring of 1907, Frank, Frances and Annie Halderman went to England and France. The Heaths travelled with them on the *S.S. Carmania*, but went their own way once they reached England. Frank and the girls stayed at Castle Hale with the St. Claire Baddelys, visited Canterbury, then crossed to France and stayed in the Hotel de France et Choiseul in Paris. They had many visits with George. "We talked, discussed and argued art with George all day."[22] George was studying at the Academie Julian and had continued his practice of studying and copying the old masters in the Louvre. He maintained a small studio at No. 3 Rue Vercingetorix and in the next few years would become a prominent, though not always popular figure, in the group of American art students in Paris.

The most detailed account of George in Paris is to be found in the autobiography of Thomas Hart Benton, and in Henry Adams' biography of Benton. The picture that Benton gives us of George is not an engaging one. "...Carlock was too much a mentor for real companionship. He was willing

to reveal his 'genius' but not to have any of its tenets questioned."[23]
However, Benton acknowledges his debt to George:

> *Carlock—a nephew of the famous Elbert Hubbard, the Roycrofter—was an erratic, somewhat inarticulate, but basically intelligent, artist, who had passed through an Impressionist phase similar to the one now engaging me and had become a disciple of Cezanne. What was more important for me, however, he had taken seriously Cezanne's directives toward Poussin and the restudy of Classical and Renaissance art. . . It was Carlock's view that more knowledge of drawing could be obtained by studying in the Louvre than in the classes of the academies. It was largely because of his promptings that I left the Academie Julian.*[24]

Adams gives a fuller and if anything less flattering picture of George. He describes him as a forbidding figure with his "wiry, uncontrollable black hair" and piercing blue-green eyes. His very inarticulateness made him seem aloof, and, when he did speak, his comments were critical, often cruel. "According to Benton's recollection, however, Carlock possessed a knowledge of art history and an intuition about the principles of modern art far beyond that of the average artist. He was a consultant for the Louvre's department of old-master drawings and a devoted advocate of Cezanne."[25] The unrelieved intensity of the man must have been trying to the younger Benton. Nevertheless, Benton continued to see a good deal of Carlock and to respect his advice. Adams tells of an incident when Benton, smarting under Carlock's criticism, challenged him to show how he would draw the subject. Carlock refused, and then realizing that Benton might suspect his inability, he said, "I'd have to work at it just like you." "The humble tone of voice as he confessed this made Tom more tolerant of his little cruelties."[26] Adams shows considerable insight, too, when he comments that Carlock, like Benton, "was probably desperately lonely, too, for he never introduced Tom to anyone."[27]

George was a loner and a perfectionist who never ceased to struggle with his craft. He was extremely secretive about his work, rarely allowing any of his fellow artists to see what he was doing. Unlike his celebrated uncle in East Aurora, words did not come easy to George. His aloofness and air of superiority were a bulwark sheltering his basic insecurity from the world. His aunt would have been sensitive to this and sympathetic. However, as his progress in art became more unconventional, more modern, even

145

Frank began to lose patience. At the same time George's confidence in himself grew. In 1910, his Uncle John paid him a visit and was pleased with the work that he saw. However, that same year his work was refused for the show at the Salon d'Automne, a blow that he was doggedly philosophical about.[28] He promised to work harder, and expressed the feeling that his aunt and uncle "ought not and can not continue to carry me through many years longer."[29] The necessity to accept help over so many years must have been humiliating, but George knew there was no other way to achieve his goal.

Written in 1911, the last letters that have come down to us from George to his aunt reflect a conflict of views and a plea for understanding, but also a determination to go his way no matter what. In January, 1911, Frank returned some dinner cards that he had designed at her request. He was hurt by her abrupt rejection. On January 27, 1911 he writes insisting that he must paint as he sees fit and not to please the public. Apparently Frank accepted this with her usual intuitive understanding. She wrote "go ahead and do it," and promised to send the allowance five days earlier.[30]

George's work in Paris continued until his death in the influenza epidemic in 1918. There was a Greenwich Village exhibit of his drawings in 1915, and Adams states that he visited the United States in 1916. Although there is no record in the family papers available, he undoubtedly saw his aunt and uncle on those visits and continued to receive their financial support. In those later years George developed a modern style that is all his own and shows evidence of great ability. His reputation among his fellow artists was considerable. Arthur Lee, whom Benton mentions as one of the group in Paris in 1909, when asked to put together "an Art Annual of the best drawings of the last 40 years," wrote:

First I thought of George Carlock, the most gifted painter, designer and draftsman among the Americans in Paris from 1906 to 1918, when he died of the flu epidemic. I knew where I could get five of his designs, one in pencil, one in pen and ink, and three made with a Japanese brush dipped in ink. Carlock may have learned his simple outline drawing from the drawings on Greek vases, but the overall rhythm he added, he had seen in Greek statues, or in the living model or learned from Ingres made drawings, for in these he achieved a unique rhythmic quality in his designs where he did most with least and we all admired his designs. He was a touchstone talisman for us.[31]

One of the two known examples of George's work that have survived is a portrait of Mrs. Arthur Lee. This is an exquisite work in the modern idiom that perfectly demonstrates the point that Lee makes about George's mastery of rhythm and line.

The story of George Carlock establishes the active involvement of John and Frances Larkin as patrons in the world of art. In commissioning the relatively unknown Frank Lloyd Wright to build his office building, John was motivated both by his regard for the opinion of his closest associates and his desire to build the best for his business family. Similarly, in supporting Frank in her many interests, whether commissioning a portrait by Selstedt, purchasing a Rosa Bonheur painting , or lending support and encouragement to young George Carlock, John demonstrated his own delight in man's creativity. He and Frank were charter members of the prestigious National Arts Club in New York, and John often went the rounds of the galleries in New York by himself.[32] He and Frank were supporters of Mr. Albright's Art Gallery in Buffalo.

Another facet of John's interest in helping others and in supporting Frank's enthusiasms is revealed in the story of the young Japanese who arrived at 237 North Street on November 19, 1906. Unfortunately there is very little information available about Masaichi Tada in the documents that have survived. There is a suggestion in the diaries that Charlie was instrumental in bringing him to Buffalo,[33] and the most specific information about Masaichi comes from Oberlin College where he attended the Academy Department in 1907–1908. On a form filled out to give information for a general catalogue of former students, Masaichi gives his local address, his home address in Japan and his date of birth—"Jan. 23rd, 1896."[34] This date of birth seems almost certainly in error, as it would make him only ten years old when he arrived in Buffalo. Photographs in the *Glencairn Log* show a mature young man who might well be twenty.

Frank first mentions Masaichi in the entry for November 18, where she notes that "Charlie had a telegram from M. T. the Japanese. He is on his way from Chicago."[35] We have already seen Frank's interest in things Japanese—the Japanese gardens at North Street and at Glencairn. Just before Masaichi's arrival she finished reading a Japanese story, "The Dragon Painter," perhaps in anticipation of his coming. On November 19, she writes "Machaichi [sic] is here, my Japanese garden poem is working out. . . a new element is here!"

Although tradition has it that Masaichi occupied a position as "house boy" in the Larkin household, the references in Frank's diaries and the pictures in the *Glencairn Log* suggest that the Japanese boy was very much a part of the family. Frank records that Christmas "was all new to him," and that she and John and the boy ushered in the New Year "in the Library waiting for Ruth. We all wished one another a Happy New Year when the whistle and the bells began."[36] She tells of discussing Buddhism with Masaichi on several occasions, of reading Lafcadio Hearn, and helping Masaichi with a poem. In the spring, he was very ill, and Frank had the doctor come and took his meals up to his room herself. At Glencairn the following summer tea was served Japanese style in the Japanese tea house. When there was a crisis with the help in August and the entire domestic staff was dismissed, Masaichi was puzzled, but happily pitched in to help Frank and Mrs. Kehr prepare the meals. Pictures in the Glencairn Log show Masaichi standing "in front of the cabin 1907," and, with Charlie's boys, preparing to plant a pine, one of several that he planted for the family before he left.

In September of 1907, Masaichi went off with Ralph Hubbard to Oberlin College. The boys came home for Christmas. Frank's diary entry for Sunday, December 29, 1907, reads, "Bertha, Ralph, Katherine here to dinner—we went to Vespers at St. Paul's—Masaichi and Matsy Yama went with us."[37] There is no further mention of Masaichi in the diaries until July of 1908, when Frank records for the 29th:

> *Wednesday—Masaichi started for Home—Japan—this morning. We all felt sad to tell him goodbye. Strange that our lives should touch that of this foreigner (he does not call himself a Christian even) and that we should grow to like and understand his better self which is refined, poetic and sincere.*

At the back of the diary in the Memoranda, she adds:

> *Masaichi has gone back to Japan. It is strange how he came into our lives and that I understood his Japanese nature. Where and when will we meet again? He waved his hat from the upper deck of the steamer Niagara river [sic] as far as he could see us. Something about his going back to the land of his birth is sad to me—and he said he was not.[38]*

Two items alone remain to close the story of Masaichi Tada. One is a formal portrait photo taken in Japan of a couple in Japanese dress. Masaichi, seated, his right arm resting on the back of his chair, holds in his lap before his kimono what looks very much like a Hubbard style broad brimmed hat. On his right stands a young woman—his wife?—holding a very western looking umbrella and apparently wearing western style shoes. The other item is a post card postmarked from Osaka, Japan, December 18, 1910. It is addressed to Mr. and Mrs. Harry Larkin, C/o Larkin Co., Buffalo, N.Y., America. The Message reads:

> *Dear Mr. and Mrs. Harry Larkin*
> *I hope you merry Christmas and new happy year*
> *Masaichi.*[39]

The story of Masaichi Tada has a very modern ring to it. The Larkins might well have been host parents for an American Field Service exchange student, if the program had existed in 1907, and it would have been characteristic of John to support such a program.

---

[1] BECHS, Larkin Soap Co. Minutes, February 26, 1900, p.19.

[2] Jack Quinan, in his *Frank Lloyd Wright's Larkin Building: Myth and Fact*, (New York:The Architectural History Foundation, 1987), gives the definitive account of the office building.

[3] Frank Lloyd Wright, *An Autobiography*, New York: Horizon Press, 1977, p.176.

[4] "Four guides are needed to attend to the visitors. From fourteen to twenty trips are made daily. The distance covered each trip is nearly a mile and requires about one hour. Visitors receive a cake of Modjeska Soap, Guest size, a sample Clover Sachet Powder and a package of printed matter." *Ourselves*, October 1, 1906.

[5] The magnesite used by Wright is often described as gray. My recollection of many visits to my father's office and to concerts in the great court is of the yellow brick and the marble-like white of the blocks of magnesite.

[6] For a full description of the Administration building and all that it provided, the reader is referred to Jack Quinan's *Frank Lloyd Wright's Larkin Building*.

[7] JDL to DDM 12/2/1899, SUNY Buffalo Archives.

[8] *Ourselves*, February 1, 1907.

[9] Quinan, *Frank Lloyd Wright's Larkin Building*, p. 62.

[10] *The Buffalo Express*, February 19, 1915, p. 6.

[11] I have not been able to determine the date when these were removed, but

assume it was not long after 1915. This incident is something that Wright's admirers are loath to discuss.

[12] FHL Diary, March 27, 1902.

[13] FHL Diary, January 21, 1902

[14] FHL Diary, January 14, February 11, 1902.

[15] FHL Diary, March 31, 1902. The "life class" was undoubtedly under the auspices of The Buffalo Fine Arts Academy of which Lars Sellstedt was one of the founders.

[16] FHL Diary, December 25, 1902.

[17] FHL Diary, December 31, 1902.

[18] George Carlock letter to FHL, July 25, 1904. These letters are in the possession of Frank Carlock's descendants.

[19] George Carlock, letter to FHL, Jan 22, 1905.

[20] FHL Diary, January 11, 1906. The Albright Art Gallery catalog lists this as an oil painting "George Carlock—#60 Hamburg Cove, N.Y." Hamburg, Connecticut, is more probably correct.

[21] FHL Diary, March 14, 1906.

[22] FHL Diary, June 16, 1907.

[23] Thomas Hart Benton, *An American in Art*, University of Kansas Press, 1969. p. 18.

[24] Ibid. p. 16.

[25] Henry Adams, *Thomas Hart Benton, Drawing from Life*, New York: Abbeville Press, 1990. p.60.

[26] Henry Adams, *Thomas Hart Benton*, New York: Alfred A. Knop, 1989. p. 42.

[27] Ibid.

[28] George Carlock, letters to FHL September 1910.

[29] George Carlock, letter to FHL October 22, 1910.

[30] George Carlock, letter to FHL February 18, 1911.

[31] Exerpt from the notes of Arthur Lee sent to me by George Carlock's nephew Basil Pollitt. The painting of Mrs. Lee is in the possession of Robert O. Muller, Lee's son-in-law.

[32] FHL diaries, *passim.*

[33] Charlie's daughter-in-law, Aline Larkin, tells me that he and Alice employed Japanese servants.

[34] Oberlin College Archives, "Special blank for students in Oberlin during the College year of 1907–08." The Academy Department would have been the equivalent of High School. His home address is given as Osato, Kaifu Gori, Tokushima Ken, Japan.

[35] FHL Diary, 11/18/1906.

[36] FHL Diary, 1/1/1907.
[37] FHL Diary, 12/29/1907. I have not been able to identify Matsy Yama.
[38] FHL Diary, 7/29/1908.
[39] Photo and postcard in author's collection.

Courtesy of the Buffalo and Erie County Public Library

The Larkin Building at the Pan American Exposition of 1901 held in Buffalo, N. Y.

Courtesy of the Buffalo and Erie County Historical Society

The inside back page of the 1905 Larkin Co. Premium List showed the Larkin Building at the Pan American Exhibition (center) and interior views of the rooms surrounding its central court that were used to display Larkin Premiums as home furnishings; and medals (upper corners and bottom center) won at national expositions by Larkin products.

East-facing side of Glencairn Hall in Queenston, Ontario, Canada, overlooking the Niagara River

Frances H. Larkin standing by the cairn, across the drive, on the west side of Glencairn Hall.

Photo from a glass negative taken by Charles H. Larkin. (Author's collection)

Frances H. Larkin in front of the Japanese Tea House and Garden at Glencairn. The Tea House was built by James A. Calvert, farm manager, in 1905. On a visit to Glencairn in the fall of 1905, Frank Lloyd Wright declared the house and garden a "great success."

Poured concrete barn on one of the Larkin Farms, built by James A. Calvert c. 1905 and still in use today. The Rumley steam tractor on the right is being used to power a machine for grinding and storing silage.

The Larkin Administration Building, designed by Frank Lloyd Wright and completed in 1906. Women employees in the photo below are wearing dresses without trains, fashionable at the time, because they had been banished as a hazard in the workplace.

A view of the Light Court in the Larkin Company Administration
Building designed by Frank Lloyd Wright. A series of inspirational
phrases and thoughts were inscribed on the front of the fifth-floor balconies. The inscription that is shown on the balcony at the top of this
photo is: ASK AND IT SHALL BE GIVEN YOU. SEEK AND YOU SHALL
FIND. KNOCK AND IT SHALL BE OPENED UNTO YOU.

THESE are the inscriptions which appear on the side-walls of the Larkin Administration Building. Take this menu home with you so you can read them over at your leisure.

ASK AND IT SHALL BE GIVEN YOU. SEEK AND YE SHALL FIND. KNOCK AND IT SHALL BE OPENED UNTO YOU.

ALL THINGS WHATSOEVER YE WOULD THAT MEN SHOULD DO TO YOU, DO YE EVEN SO TO THEM.

To Establish and Maintain	To Encourage and Reward	To Acquire and Cherish	To Inspire and Diffuse
ORDER	PURPOSE	HUMILITY	IDEAS
HARMONY	EFFORT	KNOWLEDGE	EMOTIONS
EXCELLENCE	ACHIEVEMENT	STRENGTH	INVENTIONS
GENEROSITY	CO-OPERATION	ASPIRATION	LIBERTY
ALTRUISM	ECONOMY	TRUTH	EQUALITY
SACRIFICE	INDUSTRY	NOBILITY	FRATERNITY
IMAGINATION	SINCERITY	INTEGRITY	SIMPLICITY
JUDGMENT	HUMILITY	LOYALTY	TENACITY
INITIATIVE	COURAGE	FIDELITY	STABILITY
CHEERFULNESS	FAITH	THOUGHT	INTELLIGENCE
PATIENCE	HOPE	FEELING	ENTHUSIASM
CONTENTMENT	CHARITY	ACTION	CONTROL

ADVERSITY
REFINEMENT
SYMPATHY

PRUDENCE
LEARNING
WISDOM

Visitors to the Larkin plant were given refreshments at the end of the tour and a Souvenir Menu, the inside of which is shown above. It shows the plant at the top and lists each of the inspirational inscriptions used to front the balconies on the fifth floor of the light court.

159

George Carlock in his studio in Paris. His nephew, Robert Carlock, wrote, "This is at 52 Rue l'Hamond—a dismal quarter near the Sorbonne. Very old. Dark. Cold."

Portrait of Mrs. Arthur Lee, painted by George Carlock, c. 1916.

Courtesy Robert O. Muller

Masaichi Tada, pho-
tographed after his
return to Japan. The
woman is unidenti-
fied. Note the Hub-
bard-style hat in his
hand and the
woman's western-
style shoes and um-
brella.

Seneca Indian Park
dedication, 1912,
Mrs. John Miller
Horton presiding.

Clearing Rumsey's Woods for 107 Lincoln Parkway, 1910.

Breaking ground for 107 Lincoln Parkway in 1910. From left, John D. Larkin, Jr., Frances H. Larkin, John D. Larkin, and unidentified wagon driver.

The top photo shows 107 Lincoln Parkway as it was nearing completion in 1911. The bottom photo shows it as it appeared in the Spring of 1912.

Frances H. Larkin, c. 1912

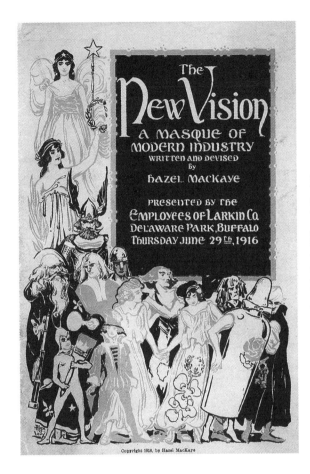

Left is the program cover for "The New Vision," a masque produced by the Larkin Company employees in Delaware Park, on June 29, 1916.

The photo below shows the cast gathered in Delaware Park.

The Dance of the Perfumes scene from "The New Vision" masque performed by Larkin Co. employees on June 29, 1916, in Delaware Park.

The Dance of the Soap Bubbles performed in front of the Great Golden Kettle (in the trees in the background) in a scene from "The New Vision" masque.

King Albert I of
Belgium visits the
Larkin Co. on October
6, 1919. Front, left to
right: John D. Larkin,
King Albert, John
Lord O'Brian, Mayor
George S. Buck.
Back, left to right:
unidentified man,
Mrs. Buck, Queen
Elizabeth, Prince
Leopold.

John D. Larkin at his desk, May 1, 1925, celebrating the 50th Anniversary of the founding of Larkin Co.

Chapter 9

The Dream Achieved 1910-1926

In February of 1909, the Buffalo newspapers were agog over "the most important real estate sale of this year."[1]

The headlines announced that John D. Larkin had purchased from the Rumsey estate "the city block fronting on Lincoln Parkway, Rumsey Road, Windsor Avenue and Forest Avenue."[2]

The *News* reported a sale price of $50,000 given on the deed and stated that both Mr. Ansley Wilcox, representing the Rumsey estate, and Mr. Larkin would make no comment beyond the fact that the deal was closed and that Mr. Larkin intended to build a home on the site. *The Buffalo Commercial* for the same date reported the sale in block headlines and expressed the belief, based on Rumsey's known asking price, that the "actual price paid was undoubtedly something more than $200,000."[3] The Commercial reporter questioned John closely about his plans for the property, and his replies, reported verbatim, are characteristic enough to deserve a place here:

> *Mr. Larkin was asked what he intended to do with the land.*
> *"I expect to build a home there," he said, "but you know that all plans are subject to change, and for that reason I would rather not speak of the matter at present."*
> *It is reported, Mr. Larkin, that several other homes are to be erected there for the use of members of your family. Is that true? he was asked.*
> *"Well, I'd rather not speak of that just now. You see I would not like to go on record as saying a thing, and then have it*

169

turn out differently. In fact, I would be better pleased if you would simply mention the transfer. The least said about it would best please me." [4]

There were numerous stipulations and restrictions written into the deed regarding the use of the land in this area known as Rumsey's Woods—the location and nature of buildings, the height of a stone wall to surround the property, and the number of residences to be built. John's purchase sparked a real estate boom in the area, and the *Commercial* reported, "Since the Larkin purchase prices have advanced to $250 a foot, and it is predicted that before the year is over all the vacant property on the parkway will be out of the market." [5] By August of 1909, the news of John's plans for his home on Lincoln Parkway appeared in all the Buffalo papers.

John and Frank had fallen in love with the heavily wooded land adjacent to Delaware Park. Here was the perfect place to build the home that Frank had been dreaming of, and here John could gather his family around him and provide the best for each of his children. They agreed from the start that the block should be known as "Larkland," and the work of clearing the land and preparing to build began without delay. The limestone wall that still surrounds the entire block must have been begun almost at once, and there is a photo dated February, 1909, which shows two men and a team of horses in the snow covered woods. Frank wrote under the photo, "First load of basswood. Hauled more to a load when snow was packed." [6] The house at 176 Windsor Avenue that John built for Frances and Harold Esty was started in the following spring or summer and was the first completed on the block. Work began on the big house at 107 Lincoln Parkway in September, but would proceed more slowly because of the great difference in scale. A photo showing John posed with shovel in hand is labeled "1st shovel full, 107 Lincoln Parkway, Septemebr 1909." Frank kept a record of the early stages of the building. On October 9, 1909, she and Ruth "took a taxicab went out to Mr. Pausch's studio to see the model in plaster of the top of our Ionic columns to be done in marble." [7] In December she reports the discovery of a giant granite boulder uncovered by the workmen digging the tunnel from the house to the garage. The stone was brought up to the surface and became a "lasting addition to the appearance of the grounds." A year later, in 1910, another boulder was discovered and placed under a tree. It had a surface so flat it could be used as a tea table. Photos taken in April of 1910 show the first floor exterior walls complete and work beginning on the second floor. One photo shows

Dr. Silas and Grandma Hubbard standing on a plank inside the marble frame of one of the French doors in what would become the dining room. The residence, designed by McCreary, Wood and Bradney, was a three-story Colonial building finished in white brick with marble trim and a large marble portico facing west to the Parkway. The drive entered from Rumsey Road on the north, curving up to a side entrance with marble steps and a graceful wrought iron and glass porte-cochère. A service wing extended east from the main body of the building, and in the L thus formed a marble terrace faced east to Windsor Avenue. On the south side of the house was a wrought iron and glass conservatory to house the plants that John and Frank loved. The ironwork was designed and executed by the Jones Iron Works, founded by George Jones who had given Levi Larkin his start in Buffalo in 1834.

The main entrance opened from the portico into a large stair hall that divided the main building symmetrically. On the right off the hall, two sets of double doors opened into the large living room with its fireplace opposite forming a bay flanked by two windows. Two tall windows at the west end of the room opened onto the portico. These, together with the windows by the fireplace, and the door leading to the conservatory flooded the room with light. To the left off the hall was first a white panelled reception room with its fireplace on the opposite wall and tall front windows looking out on the portico. Then came John's office, followed by the small household elevator that became the grandchildren's delight. Between the office and the elevator was a paneled fireplace, above which Frank would hang Lars Sellstedt's portrait of the young Dr. Silas Hubbard.[8] The paneled staircase swept up to the left beyond the elevator to a landing and then up to the second floor. Beneath the stair landing steps led down to the Rumsey Road entrance.

At the end of the hall the large dining room occupied the southeast corner of the main block of the building. There was an opening into the living room and, at the south end of the room, a door to the conservatory and a large fireplace. French doors opened east onto the terrace. The interior of the house reflected Frank's love for the elegant simplicity of the American colonial homes of the Revolutionary period that filled her scrapbooks. There was white paneling throughout except in the living and dining rooms, where the woodwork was dark. The white woodwork was beautifully finished, rubbed to a satin finish with pumice powder between each of seven coats. The mahogany doors added a warm contrast.

The second floor echoed the large hall below with the bedrooms and a sitting room opening off it. A door at the top of the stairs gave access to the servents quarters. On the third floor there was a large game room and ample storage space. In the basement, in addition to the laundry and utility rooms, there was a large white panelled ballroom.

It was a long wait before the house neared completion in January of 1912. Frank tells the story in her "Larkland" diary:

> *After many delays, promptings, pleadings and a strike at Feiste planing mill where the inside woodwork was being seasoned, we could see that a few rooms up stairs at Larkland were nearing completion. So we sent the decorator out to do the walls of two or three rooms, much to the chagrin of the finishers for no doors were hung—finally the last of the year 1911 we told them we were going to move in up stairs. Then after Christmas I went to stay with Harold and Frances at 176 Windsor Ave. and sent Butler to put the shades up. Then sent some furniture. On the twentieth of January, Mr. Larkin came out to the Esty's with Ruth & myself and brought the dogs and plenty of hand luggage. I now copy from my line a day book—Sunday January 21, 1912—Larkland at last! In the early morning we had break-fast. There had been a light fall of snow—we left the Esty breakfast table, and with our luggage & dogs, Harold and Elberta coming with us, we came here and have spent a happy day. It has been stormy and plenty of high wind—we have had log fires and dinner sent out from North St.*

> *Monday morning, 22 January—we thought the men were surprised to see us here this morning. We did not sleep as well as we will later—with sheets tacked at the doors for curtains. We are unpacking and settling and everything begins to seem homelike and nice.*

> *23 January The men are beginning to bring the doors in to hang. We have our meals brought up to the hall. We are bringing more and more from North St. It seems good that we are getting settled and that our wanderings have ceased.[9]*

So life at "Larkland" began in the winter of 1912. Within a few years, John would build three more houses: one at 160 Windsor Avenue for Harry, one at 75 Lincoln Parkway for John Jr.,[10] and one at 175 Windsor, across the street from the Estys, for Charlie and Alice. These houses were all completed by 1915, and John deeded their respective properties to each of his children in November of 1917. A service road cut through the block from Rumsey Road to Forest Avenue which provided for delivery of coal and other necessaries. In the center of the block was the large garage for 107 Lincoln Parkway with an apartment for Charles Pratt, the chauffeur, and his family, and next came the greenhouses and utility buildings. Each of the three other houses on the block had its own garage with an apartment for the chauffeur and his family, and each of the houses had its heating plant in the garage basement with a connecting tunnel for the steam pipes.

Throughout John's lifetime and after, the big house at 107 Lincoln Parkway would be a gathering place for the family: Christmas morning there were presents around the big tree in the living room; New Year's dinner brought all together in the big dining room. There were formal parties, too. Ruth's debutante ball on April 8, 1912, was a gala affair attended by 350 guests with dancing in the main hall, the dining room, and music was supplied by an orchestra "stationed behind a screen of southern palms in one end of the library."[11] The Larkins entertained "200 young people" at a ball New Year's Eve, 1914, in honor of Miss Marion Cleveland, the daughter of Frances Folsom Cleveland, the President's widow now married to cousin Tom Preston. The Prestons arrived from Princeton, N.J., on December 31, in time for the festivities, and stayed with John and Frank through the remainder of the holidays. "The house was decorated with American beauty roses, there was dancing in the reception hall and the library, and supper was served at small tables."[12] Next night there was a dinner party at "Larkland" for a small group of family and friends after which the Larkins and their guests attended the annual Charity Ball in Elmwood Music Hall where they occupied Box #28.[13] There was Ruth's wedding to Lieutenant Walter Browning Robb in the reception hall at "Larkland" on the evening of October 30, 1915, followed by a dinner and dancing for the 200 guests.[14] Shortly after the close of the first World War, the famous pianist and President of Poland, Ignace Jan Paderewski, came to Buffalo to perform at Elmwood Music Hall. His former secretary, the painter Sigismund Ivanowski, was a close friend of the Estys, and it was arranged that Mr. Paderewski would stay at 107 Lincoln Parkway while in Buffalo. "Larkland" provided a perfect setting for Frank's love of elegance and her delight in entertaining, and for John it provided a home commensurate with his position as one of Buffalo's leading citizens.[15]

Soon after the move to "Larkland," John was able to see the completion of a project that he had been nurturing for several years. He and Frank shared a keen interest in the early history of Buffalo. They were only a generation removed from the days when Buffalo was a village, vying with Black Rock for position as the chief harbor at the east end of Lake Erie. Frank's mother had taught at the school on the Seneca Indian reservation, and her father had driven his buggy out Seneca Street to treat his patients among the Indians there. The stories of Red Jacket and Mary Jemison were a part of the lore John and Frank grew up with, and the Indians were a very real presence in their world. When the former Indian burying ground on Buffam Street, just off Seneca Street, came up for sale, John and Frank were concerned that this plot of land with its sacred associations might be lost to commercial interests. To be sure, the remains of Red Jacket, Mary Jemison (the famous "white woman of the Genesee"), and some seven hundred Indians had been removed from the burying ground before the turn of the century. Nevertheless, the Larkins felt strongly that the site should be set aside as a memorial.

In 1909, John purchased the land from Allen D. Strickler and presented it to the city to be used as a memorial park. Arrangements were made to have a large granite boulder brought from the farm at Queenston, and the prominent Buffalo artist Edward Pausch was commissioned to create a bronze plaque in the shape of a wolf skin to be placed on the boulder. On June 29, 1912, an impressive ceremony of dedication took place at Seneca Indian Park. A number of prominent citizens took part in the ceremony. Mrs. John Miller Horton, a leader in civic and intellectual circles and vice president of the Niagara Frontier Landmarks association, presided, and a dedicatory talk reviewing the history of the site was delivered by Henry R. Howland. Characteristically, John remained in the background, leaving the limelight to others. Ruth Larkin, who attended with her father, unveiled the plaque, and the ceremony concluded with the singing of the national anthem and a benediction by the Reverend Edwin J. Stevens.

Frank did not attend the ceremony. Mr. Howland had sent her a copy of his talk with a note assuring her that he had reserved tickets for Dr. Hubbard and Mr. Johnston and other members of the family who might like to attend. She had apparently written to him to request the tickets and to let him know she would not be there. What kept Frank away? Perhaps she was ill, but there may be another explanation. Knowing her sympathy with everything Indian, it seems reasonable to interpret her absence as an act of protest.

All was not smooth sailing for the organizers of the event. Word of possible protest by some members of the tribes of the Seneca Indian Nation had gotten around. "Murmurings were heard which indicated that some of the younger braves were in favor of donning war paint and descending upon the crowd gathered for the ceremonies to wreck vengeance."[16] Older heads prevailed, however, and there was no war regalia. Chief Thunderwater, a chief in the Council of the Tribes, acted as spokesman for the Council, and it was planned that sixteen-year-old Floretta Poodry, daughter of Chief Poodry of the Tonawandas, would give an address at the ceremonies. However, this was not what Mrs. Horton and the organizers had in mind.

The different chieftens, who had expected to be allowed to protest the whole affair, were not included in the programme and were not even given designated seats. They, together with some of the women of the tribe, were forced to stand at a point some distance from the speakers, owing to the density of the crowd.[17]

The year was 1912, and the Civil Rights Movement a long way off. We can never know what John's feelings might have been regarding these arrangements. As usual he did what was required of him by being there as unobtrusively as possible. Let those who wanted it have the glory. For John it was enough to know that he had done what he felt was right for the Indian people. It must have been gratifying to him to know that the Indians made a point of stating to the press that, although they felt their burying ground should not have been made a public park, "they do not feel that Mr. Larkin bought their grounds and gave it for a park with any disregard for their feelings. They have only the most friendly feeling for him . . . and do not blame him in the least for their discomfort."[18]

In 1992, Allen Jemison, a descendant of Mary Jemison and a leader in the Native American community, organized a restoration of the park which had been neglected and vandalized. The bronze plaque had been stolen from the boulder, and the neglected grounds needed a good clean up. Through Allen's efforts a new plaque was made, a duplicate of the original, the grounds were cleaned and trimmed, and Seneca Indian Park was rededicated. John and Frank would have been pleased with the event. This time the Seneca Indian Nation was well represented by a descendant of Mary Jemison herself, and a group of Indian school children in full regalia. One of the group gathered around the boulder on October 23, 1992, was Norma Poodry, a niece of Floretta Poodry, who had been denied a chance to speak in 1912.

The years following the move to "Larkland" were clouded by first the threat and then the reality of war in Europe. Travel to Europe was out of the question after 1914. Frank had been able to indulge in that panacea in 1910, sailing with her friends the Kelloggs on March 5th on the *S. S. Carmania* for a cruise of the Mediterranean that called at the Azores, Madeira, Gibraltar, Genoa, Naples,and Alexandria. John had taken Ruth to England and the continent after her graduation from school in the spring of that same year. However, John's visit to England and France from May 15 to July 29, 1911, was probably his last.[19] Frank did manage one more escape from her recurring depression in the winter of 1915. Her diary, which hints darkly that "many depressing things have happened," gives no specific dates, but tells of a trip to Panama with a nurse companion, Miss Mackintosh:

> ... we sailed on the United Fruit Co. Line for Panama—so I have seen + been in Havana Cuba—have been twice at Colon—and through that most wonderful achievement of modern Times—The Panama Canal. We went through on a South American steamer and landed at half past ten at night at Balboa. We were at [blank space] a week. Went back to the beautifully situated Hotel Washington at Colon where we were for two nights and then took the same little Netapan for New York.[20]

For Frank the war meant the end of the halcyon days at Glencairn. Sometime after 1915, she bought property in East Aurora and had a modest house there where she could get away from the domestic and social pressures of the city, enjoy her chickens and her flowers, and be near her father and mother. Mary and Will Heath had built a summer place there, and Frank's land was adjacent to theirs and to a farm owned by Bert's daughter Miriam Hubbard Roelofs. Bert's son Sanford Hubbard was delighted to run the farm for his aunt, and ultimately would make the place his home.

John maintained his interest in the Canadian farms and was as absorbed in the business as ever. Larkin Co. continued to thrive through the war years. In 1912 the big warehouse buildings—R, S, and T—were built to provide storage and shipping space for the premiums and products. The three buildings are actually one unit, the ground floor of which served as a railroad terminal where incoming and outgoing shipments could be handled. Two railroad spurs ran into the building at its east end, serving loading platforms 580 feet long that ran the length of the building. The company maintained its own oil-burning locomotive, "powerful enough to haul a train of 30 standard freight cars,"[21] to bring shipments from the surrounding railroad yards. "Larkin the First," as the engine was proudly dubbed, handled freight not only for the terminal warehouse, but for "P" building on the other side of Van Rensselaer Street as well.

Sales through the war years remained steady, averaging close to $20 million between 1912 and 1920. John must have felt great satisfaction that his business had reached such a plateau, but there was no let up in his desire to see the company grow in service at home and abroad. Even before the United States entered the conflict in Europe, many of the men in the company entered the armed services. In June, 1916, the Directors passed a resolution that employees called into military service be retained on the payroll until January 1, 1917, and assured of their position with the company on their return.[22] Officers and employees of the company also served the government in civilian capacities. On April 6, 1917, the United States declared war on Germany, and in May, Darwin D. Martin was called to Washington where he served on the Purchasing Committee of the Council of National Defense until late January, 1918.[23] From the start, the company did its share in the war effort, purchasing $100,000 of Liberty Bonds, supplying soap and other products for the Army, wrapping bandages and sending supplies for the Red Cross.

Long before the United States became actively involved in the European conflict, the war struck home to John and Frank with the loss of Elbert Hubbard in the sinking of the *Lusitania*. In her *Glencairn Log*, Frank tells of going to Toronto with Ruth and Walter on the last day of April, 1915. At the King Edward Hotel and everywhere there were soldiers in uniform, "a subdued air pervaded the streets and shops—and word was received that ninety Canadian officers had been killed, wounded and missing at a battle with the Germans in France."[24] Undoubtedly Frank knew of Bert's plans to sail for Europe and his self-appointed mission to end the war in Europe. Although relations with Bert had been strained since the events of 1902, there had never been a complete break with East Aurora. The ties with the family there were too strong, and time had healed some of the hurt. On the morning of May 1st, the date the *Lusitania* was to sail, Frank was "very much depressed" and, cutting her stay in Toronto short, returned to Glencairn "jarred and half ill." Of course, she would have known of the warnings that the Germans had issued against sailing on the *Lusitania*, and Tom Gadsby, the manager at Glencairn, told her next day of the reports in the papers of Bert's interviews on shipboard before sailing. He had boasted that, "if he was aboard the Lusitiania when she was torpedoed, he would be able to do justice to the Kaiser' in his writings"[25] Clearly Frank felt a sense of doom in her brother's overweening confidence. The entry in the Log concludes:

On Friday, May 7th at half past two o'clock off the coast

of Ireland the Lusitania *was torpedoed. She sank off of Kinsala—about ten miles from the shore. Eleven Hundred were lost. We never have heard from Elbert. I have been at E. Aurora most of the time since.*[26]

There was, of course, nothing Frank could do but to console her parents and share their grief with sister Mary and with Bertha, Katherine and the boys. John, however, lost no time in seeking first hand informaton about the fate of the Hubbards. News of the disaster reached the evening papers on Friday May 7th, and, on Monday the 10th, John sent several cables to Mr. John Allen who lived on the outskirts of London in Purley, Sussex. Mr. Allen was probably known to John through the business, and his letters tell us that he had visited the Larkins in Buffalo and had gone to East Aurora where he had met Elbert Hubbard, but not Alice. Allen went directly to the Cunard office in London.

I took with me a note asking for particulars and stating I could identify Mr. H, and I posted duplicate to L'pool office and similar one to Queenstown. . . How little I thought when I went out to East Aurora and made the acquaintance of Mr. Hubbard, and was accompanied round the place by him, to what purpose my knowledge of him might be put. I am glad now I went.[27]

Next day Allen travelled to Liverpool, where he was told pictures of the victims would be available at the Cunard office. However, when they failed to materialize, he decided to cross the Irish channel to Queenstown in spite of his wife's fears of German submarines. In the cove behind the Cunard office he witnessed first hand the terrible effects of the disaster: the lifeboats beached, the railings draped with lifebelts taken from the bodies of the drowned, the yard filled with coffins, and the room inside "devoted to the exposure of the bodies last come in and still uncoffined."[28] Allen made the acquintance of William H. Harkness, an Assistant Purser on the *Lusitania* who was among the survivors. Harkness had known the Hubbards on shipboard and would be able to make an identification on the basis of his own knowledge as well as from the photographs and descriptions that Allen gave him. Allen also had Harkness make a sworn declaration before the American Vice Consul that might help in probate matters. An old acquaintance of Allen's, Mr. Hoblyn, deputy manager of the Cunard office in Liverpool, was in Queenstown and arranged for Allen to examine all the trinkets and jewelry found on the bodies. He found nothing to answer the descriptions John had given him. On the night of May 14, Allen left the grisly scene behind him.

I would not leave so soon but the features of the bodies coming in now are becoming difficult of recognition and decomposed bodies cannot be embalmed.[29]

He closed the letter with a promise to write to "the nephew in Italy,"—George Carlock. On May 28th Allen wrote to John enclosing a letter from Harkness who had returned the photos and declared the search hopeless. Allen's last letter to John, written June 4th, 1915, enclosed a reply from George Carlock, and expressed his dismay at the failure of Britain to prepare sooner for the German threat and his hope that the United States will stay out of the actual fighting, "but break off relations with the German outlaws."[30]

As we have seen, in spite of the war in Europe, business at home continued to thrive, and Larkin Co. occupied a unique place in American business, reaching from coast to coast with its "Factory to Family" method of bringing quality goods to the average household. The war years saw considerable expansion and diversification in the business: Buffalo Leather Goods was acquired in 1915, the Larkin Gasoline business and the manu-facture of women's and children's apparel came in 1917, chain stores to market groceries and Larkin products were opened in Buffalo and Peoria in 1918. One need only look through the copies of *Ourselves* for these years to feel the wonderful sense of belonging, the personal pride in the company, the high morale that existed among the Larkin employees. John had indeed created a business family.

In June, 1916, before the U.S. entered the war, the Larkin Co. employ-ees staged an elaborate pageant in Delaware Park for the benefit of their families and friends and five hundred sales contest winners brought to Buffalo by the company to receive their rewards. "The New Vision: A Masque of Modern Industry" was written by Hazel Mackaye, with music by John Lund, and its theme was the triumph of Imagination over the forces of Ignorance in industry.

In the best allegorical tradition of the masque, "The New Vision" dramatized the virtues of enlightened cooperative work that we have seen exemplified in the inscriptions on the office building. Industry, the central figure in the allegory, is summoned by the Creative Energies of the World to serve mankind. Mistakenly he accepts Ignorance as his ally in the management of his Elemental Forces—Steam, Electricity, Machinery and Labor. The result is chaos, and the tyranny of Ignorance, with his forces of Disorder, Sloth, Greed and Strife, threatens to destroy the Elemental Forces. When Industry sees how bad a master Ignorance is, he begs for another spirit to come to his aid. Imagination appears, and Ignorance and his Hosts are banished. Imagination calls up her Spirits of Order, System, Ambition, Service and Co-operation. Industry and his forces swear allegiance to Imagination, and with her aid they are able to create wonders for mankind. They raise a Golden Kettle from which emerge to dance upon the green, first, the Maid of the Mist, followed by soap bubbles and then by the fragrant perfumes. Imagination summons Science and Research, the Kettle boils again bringing forth Colors and an Elf to mix them. Perched on a giant paint pot, he mixes the Colors in an intricate dance. Then follows the Pageant of Products representing twenty-two countries which contribute to the making of the Larkin Products. Finally, the citizens of the World of Men are summoned to choose gifts from the Magic Wish Box (shades of Elbert Hubbard's Combination Box!), Co-operation and Service summon the Larkin Workers and "Imagination bids all assembled to sing America..."[31]

The preparations for this ambitious piece occupied many weeks and required the skills of men and women from every branch of the business. After arrangements had been made with the city authorities for the use of the site in Delaware Park, E.G. Green, the company engineer, and his staff surveyed the area and made maps for the use of the Pageant Committee. The chosen site was the south east corner of the park reached through the gate at Rumsey Road and Delaware Avenue. Here there is a level open area bordered on the north and west by trees and shrubs beyond which the land slopes sharply down to the lake. The trees formed a natural theatrical drop and wings, and the sharp drop beyond made it possible for the players to make their entrances and exits effectively. This was important with a cast of more than five hundred. Under Green's supervision, bleachers were erected facing the playing area to accommodate the five hundred secretaries from all over the country who were winners of the annual sales contest, as well as the families and friends of the participants—an audience of several thousand.[32]

In addition to providing for the playing area and the seating, the engineers were responsible for the special effects required, particularly the Golden Kettle with its clouds of steam.

The steam boiler, which made the Golden Kettle boil, was particularly intractable, and caused much worry on the part of everyone. Boiler No. 1

did not steam fast enough. Boiler No.2 developed a leaky tube at the dress rehearsal, and gasped out a most pitiful steam cloud. Finally it behaved most beautifully at the performance.[33]

The costumes were designed by Alex O. Levy of the Art Department. Mr. Levy went to New York to acquire the costumes for the principals, and supervised the making of the costumes for the dancers and attendant characters. The Pageant of Products, with its international flavor was a particular challenge, and everyone pitched in to beg, borrow or create the various ethnic garments required. Alex Levy personally supervised the dyeing of the costumes that the Muslin Underwear Department created for the dancers using sample dyes that had accumulated over the years in the Research Laboratory. Many properties, too, were called for: balloons for the Soap Bubbles, a dancing Paint Pot and dancing Perfume Bottles, battery powered spinning wheels, and the Magic Wish Box.

After months of preparation, Thursday, June 29th dawned gray and threatening rain. However, after an 11 o'clock shower the clouds parted, and "the programme was carried out under a gray and blue sky." Prizes were awarded to the contest winners, "the first four of the 500 receiving Ford automobiles."[34] The sixty piece orchestra under the direction of John Lund struck up the music, and the presentation of the masque unfolded without a hitch.

This theatrical event affords one more example of the feeling of solidarity and pride in their organization that characterized the Larkin employees. Thumbing through the pages of *Ourselves*, one wonders how the Larkinites found time to conduct the thriving business that bound them all together. There were numerous YWCA activities, the Womens' Fife and Drum Corps, the Mens' Club, the athletic teams, field days and picnics, dramatic presentations, concerts and radio broadcasts, not to mention such visiting speakers as Billy Sunday, Wilfred Grenfell, and Booker T. Washington.

One of the most impressive events in the annals of John's company took place just after the close of World War I, when King Albert of Belgium visited Buffalo and made a tour of the Larkin factories on October 6, 1919. The king, who had won the respect and devotion of the allies for his courageous stand against the German Kaiser, was eager to expedite the recovery of his little country from the ravages of the war. He came to the United States primarily for the purpose of studying American business and manufacturing methods. King Albert was accompanied by Queen Elizabeth and Crown Prince Leopold, who, though only just eighteen, had already distinguished himself in the defence of his country. The royal party was to travel from Boston to San Francisco, making only one major stop on the way west at Niagara Falls and Buffalo. The two main points of interest in Buffalo were the Pierce Arrow plant and the Larkin manufacturing plant.

Buffalo was ready for them. Mayor Buck, Col. William J. Donovan, John Lord O'Brian and the rest of the city dignitaries who formed the reception committee were dressed in their top hats and cutaways when they assembled at the Terrace Station to await the arrival of the royal train from Niagara Falls. Following a late arrival and the formal reception, the royal party was taken to the Goodyear home on Delaware Avenue for refreshments before the tour of the city began. Finally the motorcade set out up Delaware Avenue. Students from Lafayette High School cheered them at Chapin Parkway on their way out to the Pierce Arrow plant. After the reception there, the route took them through Delaware Park to Humboldt Park where the students of Masten Park High cheered them on their way to the Larkin factory complex. There the Larkin Girls Drum Corps greeted the royal party with a rousing rendition of the Belgian national anthem.[35]

Seneca Street was lined with spectators and the employees in the office and the factory were ready and waiting. Cheers went up as the six-foot-six figure of the king in the uniform of a lieutenant general of the Belgian Army assisted his diminutive queen from the car and proceeded through the gate to the steps of the office building. At the top of the steps, their host stood alone to greet them, his white hair and beard in bright contrast to his formal black attire. After Mayor Buck's introductions, John took over as host and conducted the tour, first through the office building and then through the factory. The *Courier* pointed out next day that "the longest stop of the party was made at the Larkin plant."[36] John must have felt great satisfaction as he took them from his world famous office building through the various sections of the plant—the food processing, the garment manufacturing the stamping and packaging of Sweet Home soap. Time was limited, but, in spite of constant pressure from the secret service men to move on, the King and Queen were determined to see this striking example of manufacturing expertise. They were impressed by the "immensity of the operations," by the "two hundred power-driven machines [in the sewing room] in operation at the same time, and in a large spacious room that was supplied abundantly with the maximum of fresh air, light and comfort"[37] that bore no resemblance to the sweat shop conditions often associated with garment manufacturing. Following the inspection of the Sweet Home soap stamping, packaging and wrapping process, the tour ended. The party descended to Seneca Street, King Albert took leave of his host with a warm handshake, and, amid the cheers of the crowd, the cavalcade of cars moved on toward the center of the city.

A few days later, John received a letter from Mayor Buck that gave him a sense of real satisfaction:

> *To me the approach of the party to your great office building was one of the most dramatic incidents of the whole trip about the city. As you stood alone upon the steps, the great walls of the plant which you have created towered about you and stood as an impressive monument to your industry and business ability. You have done much to build up Buffalo and yesterday you helped again to lend distinction to the city in the impression which you left upon the minds of our guests.[38]*

These years after the tensions of the war brought John many satisfactions and at the same time disappointments. In 1919 a plan that John had favored earlier in the company's history was revived. The July 25, 1919, issue of *Ourselves* was devoted to a proposal to the employees by the current stockholders of Larkin Co. of a plan "opening the way to co-operative ownership with its employees..."[39] Like The New Vision, this stock sharing plan would promote the ideals of co-operation, industry and integrity that John had always sought to foster among his fellow workers. The opening paragraphs of his announcement of the plan in *Ourselves* express his views simply and eloquently:

> *It has always been a great source of happiness to both the Directors of this Company and to myself that the atmosphere of our organization has rather been that of a united family than of a business institution. This spirit of mutual helpfulness and affection has been without question the cornerstone of our success.*
>
> *You may imagine then with what genuine satisfaction I announce to the Employees of this Company an important proposal on the part of the present Stockholders whereby the Employees will become in actuality part owners of this business and sharers in its benefits and profits.[40]*

In actual fact, this plan never really got off the ground, and ultimately was scrapped, as its predecessor had been in the 1890s. The first co-operative ownership plan had originated at the time of the formation of the first corporation—The Larkin Soap Manufacturing Co. In January of 1892, an offer was made to sell stock in the new company to qualified employees and customers. Referring to the newly adopted method of Factory to Family, the announcement stated:

> *We have long believed in this principle that underlies all cooperative industries, viz: that the producer and the consumer should join hands, and that the faithful employee and the loyal patron should share justly in the benefits which they have helped to create.*[41]

For reasons that are not clear in the record this early plan was soon abandoned, and within a few years John and Darwin Martin, and perhaps others of the Directors, bought back the stock that had been sold. This was a period of tremendous expansion, and probably the principal owners felt threatened with a loss of control over policy and management. There is no way to tell who first conceived of the plan—Larkin, Hubbard or Martin, but it is certain that it would never have been introduced without John D. Larkin's approval. It would be characteristic of John to welcome the combination of practical business considerations with the humanitarian concept of benefiting both customers and employees.

In 1919, the same would be true of this second plan for co-operative ownership. It would enlist the interest and loyalty of the employee by giving him a stake in the ownership of the business, thus ensuring his best effort. In addition the plan would increase the workers income and finally provide for his retirement. Johanna Oreskovich points out:

> *This provision stipulated that after twenty-five years of service, or age 65 for women and 70 for men, the employee would receive a pension consisting of the regular dividend on his stock plus an additional 5% dividend throughout the remainder of his life-time.*[42]

Darwin Martin was responsible for drawing up the plan which apparently met with the approval of the Directors and was enthusiastically announced in *Ourselves* with glowing articles of recommendation by D.D. Martin, W.R. Heath, H.M. Esty, Charles Larkin and John Jr. as well as endorsements by managers and employees. As Ms. Oreskovic points out in her excellent article there were negative responses from the start. There was considerable apathy among the lower wage earners. The plan for peer election of eligible employees became a source of discussion, and there was fear that the stock distribution would be used to forestall wage increases.[43] Almost at once the Directors began to feel threatened by the fear that the managers of the various departments would use the stock offer as a means of gaining power.

The result of all this was that no real action was taken to implement the plan, and a year later, July 7, 1920, John D. Larkin Jr. proposed a revision of the plan which eliminated the pension feature and substituted profit sharing for the co-operative ownership of the original plan. As Ms Oreskovich points out this "cut away the philosophical foundations on which the Plan had been built,"[44] Martin and Heath argued forcefully against the new plan and urged the implementation of the original plan. However, the Board approved the revised plan which was ratified by the employees and put in operation in January of 1921. It was abandoned before the year was out. There is no record of why, but the severe drop in sales from $31,675,000 in 1920 to $18,890,200 in 1921 must certainly have been a factor.

The years 1919–1925 marked many changes in the history of John's company and his family. At the Company the battle over the co-operative ownership plan defined a serious split in management. As we have seen, John always saw the business as a family affair and from the start intended that his sons would take over the role that he had played from its inception. During the war years, Charlie lost interest in pursuing the career his father had laid out for him. In 1917, his wife Alice had moved to California and he wanted to be with her there. He was torn between the polarities of business and family. His real interests were, like his mother's, literary and philosophical, and he longed to pursue them. By 1919, Charlie persuaded his father that he really must move, and whatever John's disappointment may have been, he sent his son on his way with his blessing and an independent income.

John Jr. had been assuming more responsibility during these years, and Charlie's departure placed him in the position of successor to the presidency of the Company. Unlike his brothers, John Jr. was a gregarious man who enjoyed the social advantages that his position as his father's successor afforded. He had some of his uncle Bert's flair for the limelight, and entered actively into playing host to the annual Travel Party for the prize winning Club Secretaries, presiding at banquets for members of the branch sales forces, and maintaining a prominent place in Buffalo society. As we have seen, the Co-operative Ownership Plan pitted John Jr. against his father's two most valued associates, Darwin Martin and William Heath. "Dar" had been with John almost from the start, and Will was John's brother-in-law. John must have seen what was happening, but his commitment to the ideal of a family business was paramount. With Charlie gone, only John Jr. and Harry and his two sons-in-law remained to carry on the business as he envisioned it. At seventy five John must have welcomed John Jr.'s willingness to take on more of the responsibilities for Company operations, and if there was growing friction between John Jr. and Martin and Heath, John would have tended to minimize it. Indeed he may have been unaware of the tension, sheltered from it by a growing protectiveness of their aging father on the part of his children.

In the spring of 1922, John suffered the loss of his beloved Frank. Her health had always been a matter of concern, and for the past two years she had fought a loosing battle against illness. In spite of ups and downs Frank had lived a full and active life. Although she and John had often been apart because of business and travel, theirs had been a very close relationship. Very different in temperament, they complemented each other. Frank filled his life with the excitement and wonder of art and literature and romance. John provided the serenity and the security that she needed to fulfill herself. Although there were times when she felt abandoned by John's preoccupation with his business affairs and scorned the gold pieces that he gave her instead of flowers one anniversay,[45] she welcomed the lifestyle that his business acumen provided and relied always on his unfailing good judgment, his gentle affection and constant concern for her welfare. The end came on April 15, 1922, at "Larkland," and Frank was buried in Forest Lawn Cemetery beside Edith and "baby" Hubbard and her father Dr. Silas Hubbard. Her mother, Juliana Frances Hubbard would survive her, dying at age 95 in 1924.

After Frank's death, Ruth and Walter Robb moved into 107 Lincoln Parkway with their children, Elizabeth and the baby, John.[46] It was a great comfort to John to have his daughter assume the management of the household, and he welcomed the presence of the children. His business obligations kept him fully occupied as always. Every morning Charles Pratt would drive him downtown, first to the office of the Title & Mortgage Company, which he had founded in 1916 and in which he was the principal stockholder, and then to the office on Seneca Street. At five o'clock he would return home, take off his shoes and lie down for a nap before dinner at six. Evenings were devoted to reading the papers and to playing with the children. Elizabeth remembers his teaching her to play cards—rummy and double solitaire. Life continued much as usual, and few would have guessed the extent of the empty space that Frank's death had left in his life. Sometimes in the evening or on Sundays John would walk up the Parkway to Soldier's Place to see Mother Hubbard, who lived in the Frank Lloyd Wright house with sister Mary and Will Heath. Often they would sit without communicating except in that unspoken way two people have who have known and loved and lost much that they both treasured.

In June of 1924, William Heath left Larkin Company, selling his stock to John D. Larkin, Inc., the holding company which had been formed the year before to handle John's assets. At the same time Harold Esty was gravely ill. His illness and death would cloud the 50th anniversary celebration the following spring. However, in spite of changes and losses the company forged ahead toward the celebration of the "Fifty Golden Years." At the age of 79, John was still at his desk every day and looking forward to the big day in May. Business was booming again after the slump in the early 20s, and Larkin Company was expanding its retail outlets with a Department Store on Seneca Street and a store in Chicago purchased from Julius Oppenheimer. At the same time, the Company was playing a role in Buffalo's cultural as well as business life. The Larkin Orchestra presented concerts over radio station WGR on Friday nights from 10 to 11 p.m. In April, 1925, John announced his gift to the employees of an organ to be installed in the office building for their relaxation and pleasure during working hours. The instrument, one of the largest in the country, was "a Moller Concert Organ, with four manuals and pedals, 101 independent stops, and will use in all 7396 pipes. It will include two sets of chimes, two harps, and a Steinway Concert Grand Piano."[47] The organ would not be complete until some time after the big day, but to the employees it was the crowning gift from their beloved founder.

As we have seen, the celebration of the Fifty Golden Years, May 1, 1925, went smoothly. With summer came the return to Glencairn where Ruth and her family had renewed the old patterns, and there were visits to Harry and John Jr. and Frances on the Lake Shore. John's interest in all the family was keen, and he especially enjoyed being surrounded by his grandchildren and sharing in their interests. Autumn came and with it John's 80th birthday, September 29, 1925. Christmas, with its festivities at the office and at home was a favorite time and a happy one that year. The organ in the office provided Christmas carols much to the delight of the employees, and at "Larkland" the family gathering around the big tree was a particularly happy one. The winter cold was no barrier to John's regular attendance at the office, but in mid-January the routine was broken by illness.

John was laid up with an attack of the grip, but after several days seemed to make a complete recovery. "He was able to go out, and on February 5 was guest at a dinner party and appeared to enjoy himself thoroughtly throughout the evening."[48] However, a few days later John suffered a relapse and was confined again to his bed. The News article quaintly refers to "weakness" and "sinking spells." In spite of the best care, the illness persisted, and the end came quietly about 1 P. M. on Monday, February 15, 1926. The papers had followed the course of his illness, and John's death was received with many public expressions of grief and of admiration for one of Buffalo's great citizens. John's role as a business leader, his many charities (including $240,000 to the YMCA and large endowments for the University of Buffalo and Lafayette College), and his personal qualities of calm reasonableness, constructive thinking and clearness of vision were noted and extolled.

The funeral service was conducted in the home on Lincoln Parkway by an old friend, Bishop Charles H. Brent, and was attended by the family, close business associates and friends. The list of bearers included such well known Buffalo names as D. D. Martin, Wm. Heath, George F. Rand, E. J. Barcalo, John Lord O'Brian, Norman E. Mack, Edward H. Butler, George B. Mathews, Joseph H. Morey, Ansley Wilcox, and Elbert and Sanford Hubbard.[49] John was buried beside Frank in the lot in Forest Lawn Cemetery that he had purchased that summer of 1885 when Edith died.

The editorial comment in the *Buffalo Evening News* the day following John's death perhaps best sums up the place that he held in the eyes of his fellow citizens:

> *The share that Mr. Larkin had in building Buffalo is greater than is generally known, for he was unostentatious in all his activities. He gave generously for the advancement of education in the city and contributed largely to all local benevolences. He always showed concern for the betterment of his fellows, always was ready and eager to advance projects which promised to advance the interests of the community. In every way he was a fine type.*[50]

The life of John Durrant Larkin is an American success story in the best sense of the term. It is the story of a man devoted to his family and his community who pursued a career in business not only for himself, but for what that business could contribute to the well being of others. He was a man who enjoyed his work, who knew how to play, who always avoided the limelight, and whose greatest satisfactions came from his human contacts at work and at home.

---

1 *Buffalo News*, February 6, 1909, p,10.
2 Ibid., February 4, 1909, p. 1.
3 *Buffalo Commercial*, February 4, 1909, p.1.
4 Ibid.
5 *Buffalo Commercial*, February 19, 1909, p.4.
6 Photo album owned by Elizabeth Robb Duane.
7 FHL, "Larkland" Diary, 1909–1912. Edward L.A. Pausch was a prominent Buffalo artist who had made the death mask of President McKinley.
8 The Sellstedt portrait of Silas Hubbard is in the collection of the East Aurora Historical Society at the Elbert Hubbard Museum in East Aurora, N.Y.
9 Ibid. Here Frank's "Larkland" Diary ends, with the exception of a newspaper clipping describing the ball given in the new home to introduce Ruth into society.
10 This house, now known as "Larkin House," is owned by the Buffalo Seminary.
11 *The Buffalo Courier*, April 9, 1912, p.5. The room referred to as "the library" was always called "the living room" by the family.
12 *The Buffalo Courier*, Friday January 1, 1915, p.5.
13 *Buffalo Evening News*, January 2, 1915, p.3.
14 *Buffalo Evening News*, November 1, 1915. p. 7.
15 The big house at 107 Lincoln Parkway is gone, torn down in 1939, a victim of the Depression and the war years. All of the other "Larkland" houses remain much as they were.
16 *The Buffalo Courier*, June 30, 1912, p.1.
17 Ibid.
18 *Buffalo Express*, June 30, 1912, p.29.
19 FHL, *Glencairn Log*, pp. 81-82.
20 Ibid., p.90.
21 "Marion Harland," *My Trip Thru The Larkin Factories*, Buffalo, N.Y.: Larkin Co., 1913, p.62.
22 Larkin Co. Minutes, p.183.
23 Ibid., p. 192.
24 FHL, *Glencairn Log*, p. 91. The battle referred to is probably the second battle of Ypres, 4/22–5/25, in which for the first time the Germans used chlorine gas against the allied troops.

[25] *The Boston Globe*, Saturday, May 8, 1915, p.3.

[26] FHL, *Glencairn Log*, p.92.

[27] OL, John Allen to John D. Larkin, May 10, 1915. In the author's collection.

[28] OL, J.A. to J.D.L., May 14, 1915.

[29] Ibid.

[30] OL J.A. to J.D.L., June 4, 1915.

[31] Program for "The New Vision: A Masque of Modern Industry" by Hazel Mackaye, 1916. In author's collection.

[32] *Buffalo Express*, June 30, 1916, quoted in *Ourselves*, July 15, 1916, p. 11.

[33] Ibid., p. 4.

[34] Ibid., p. 11.

[35] *The Buffalo Courier*, October 7, 1919, p. 5.

[36] Ibid., p. 14.

[37] *Ourselves*, November 1, 1919, p. 3.

[38] Ibid., p. 2.

[39] *Ourselves*, July 25, 1919, p. 9.

[40] Ibid., p.1.

[41] Four page folder sent to customers, January 25, 1892, BECHS Larkin Collection Bound Vol. #1.

[42] Johanna Oreskovic, "The Co-operative Ownership Plan of the Larkin Company, 1919–1921," *Studies in History*, Vol.3, SUNY at Buffalo, 1981–1982, p.59.

[43] Ibid., p. 60

[44] Ibid., p. 62.

[45] FHL, Diary, May 10, 1907.

[46] The Robbs had been living in the house that John built for Charlie and Alice at 175 Windsor Avenue which they purchased when Charlie moved to California.

[47] *Ourselves*, April 24, 1925, p.1.

[48] *Buffalo Evening News*, February 15, 1926, p. 1.

[49] *Buffalo Express*, February 18, 1926, p. 4. The paper gives the complete list of honorary and active bearers.

[50] *Buffalo Evening News*, February 16, 1926, p. 8.

Epilogue

During the days of his last illness, John D. Larkin must have felt great satisfaction in the knowledge that the business that he and his associates had built was firmly established in an expanding economy and would undoubtedly continue to thrive indefinitely. John's business ventures had survived the Panic of 1893, steered a safe course through the war years and come out on top after severe losses in the recession of 1921–1922. The beginning of the boom in 1923 brought profits that wiped out what looked like a $900,000 loss the first half of that year, and from that point on there seemed to be no limit. The departure of William Heath and Darwin Martin might have raised questions in John's mind, but he would have felt confident that his boys could carry on successfully.

What John could probably never have realized was that his dream of a benevolent paternalism that would serve the interests of his family, his employees and the community was already something of an anachronism in 1926. In the years to come the forces of change would wreak havoc with this simple idealism and its vision of a cooperative interchange between producer and consumer. The revolutions in transportation and communication, the changes in manufacturing and merchandising techniques, the social changes in the status of women and the organization of labor, and the disastrous economic conditions that followed the stock market crash of 1929 all contributed to the decline in sales that brought Larkin Co Inc. and its subsidiaries down between 1925 and 1940. In retrospect, the wonder is that the business survived on its momentum as long as it did. There is no question but that one of the strongest reasons for this survival was the backlog of good will that the company had built up over the years. Throughout the country, wherever there was a Larkin Secretary running a Larkin Club, there was great loyalty and an unshakable belief in the integrity of the company, its management and its products.

During the years following John D. Larkin's death the company continued to thrive. Home craft stores specializing in unfinished furniture, wall paper, painter's supplies, etc. were opened in Rochester and Syracuse. Household storage with dustproof, fireproof rooms made R, S & T buildings "the first public, government-bonded warehouse in the city of Buffalo."[1] In 1928, the company closed its books "with the largest year's business in its history" according to an article in New York Women's Wear.[2] The Larkin Market opened on Seneca Street in 1929, and the Larkin Bakery also began operation to supply the market and chain stores with baked goods.[3] In 1930, total sales showed only a small drop from the year before,[4] and a Larkin Gas Station was opened at the corner of Van Rensselaer and Seneca Streets. The company seemed to be riding out the depression that gripped the country, but this was not to last. On December 3, 1931, Larkin Co Inc. paid its last dividend. From then on it was all down hill.

In 1932, the company lost over a million dollars, and over the next five years the losses ran between five and eight hundred thousand dollars annually. Little was done, however, in the face of these losses during the 1930s to adjust the business to the changes, to curtail expenses and to adapt to changing manufacturing methods. The old four-story soap kettles were already dinosaurs in their field. Furthermore, the company had long since diversified its activities in manufacturing and sales to such an extent that soap had become secondary to the vast assortment of merchandise offerings in the catalog. Yet the management under John D. Larkin Jr., perhaps blinded by the intense loyalty of Larkin customers, seemed to be committed to maintaining the business without change as John had envisioned it. Finally in 1936, the manufacture of soap was discontinued altogether, and the last soaps for the catalog were manufactured by the A. Harris Soap Co.

By 1938, the majority of the stockholders recognized that drastic measures were required. John Jr. had been taken ill and was confined to his home. His brother Harry represented him at the office and spent every evening in conference with him at his home. The situation became increasingly awkward, and the creditors increasingly insistent. On expert advice from some of Buffalo's best corporation lawyers, the owners decided in 1938 to separate the company into several corporate entities and to apply for a Reconstruction Finance Corporation loan in order to avoid bankruptcy. Kenland, Inc., formed to handle the company's real estate, and Larkin Warehouse Inc. (R,S & T buildings) were organized as separate companies. In January, 1939, Harry H. Larkin was elected president of the companies by the majority of the stockholders represented by Charles H. Larkin, Frances Esty and Ruth L. Robb. At the same time, the Larkin Store was moved from across Seneca Street into the Administration Building at considerable expense. Crate Larkin, in charge of the store, insisted on bringing in an outside firm rather than using the company maintenance staff to effect the move.[5] In October, the Administration Building was sold by Kenland to Larkin Co Inc., and, in December, the RFC, which had refused to make a loan to Larkin Co Inc., granted a loan to Larkin Warehouse to purchase RS&T buildings from Larkin Co Inc. The last catalog of Larkin Co Inc., #124, was issued in 1940, and in that year John Jr. and his son Crate both resigned their positions with the company.

A Creditors' Committee was established in the spring of 1941 to represent the firms to which the company was in debt, and immediately steps were taken to cut back. The payroll was cut from $20,000 per month to $700 per month within a year, and Harry and Walter Robb served without compensation for several years after February, 1942. The Larkin Gasoline Company was sold to Gulf Oil, the Philadelphia and Peoria Branches were closed, and two new companies were formed: The Larkin Store Corporation, to carry on mail order and store sales, and Larkin Products Inc. to continue the greatly curtailed manufacture of products. To make room for new uses of the factory buildings, the giant soap kettles were dismanteled by the maintenance department and cut up to be sold for scrap

A detailed account of the measures that were used to save the Larkin interests from bankruptcy is to be found in a report prepared in 1945 for the stockholders by Walter F. Winters.[6] There is no need here to review all the intricacies of these transactions. Suffice it to say that in 1943 all creditors had been paid off, and that over the next few years all customer claims against the company were settled. Surely this was as John would have wanted it.

One of the problems Kenland and the Warehouse faced in breaking up the real estate of the company was the fact that the powerhouse supplied heat and steam to all the buildings in the complex, not just to the central block of factory buildings known as Unit 2. Long term leases in Unit 2 made the sale of the property as a whole virtually impossible. In 1943, after lengthy negotiations, the government exercised its power of condemnation and took over Unit 2 and the powerhouse for use by the Armed Services.[7] Larkin Warehouse built its own heating plant, and other properties were left to fend for themselves.

A matter of considerable concern to many in recent years has been the fate of the Frank Lloyd Wright Office Building which was torn down in 1950 after years of neglect. Two things happened to that building which ultimately rendered its preservation impossible: it was sold to a buyer who abandoned it, and it was badly vandalized. In 1943, L. B. Smith, a construction firm in Harrisburg, PA., purchased Larkin Co Inc. to use its liabilities to offset profits, and the office building was the company's sole physical asset. Smith had no use for the building. Much of its contents were sold off, including the organ,[8] and the building was left vacant. It stood unoccupied, without heat through the war years, during which time it was stripped of any metal that could be sold for scrap, its windows were broken, and it was generally rendered unusable. The City of Buffalo, which had taken the property over for back taxes, made a number of attempts to sell the building, advertising nation wide. Finally a trucking firm offered $5,000 and undertook to tear down the building, a job that turned out to be disastrously difficult.

By 1950 the Larkin companies were on their feet again. The Warehouse had become the mainstay of the business and, in turn, housed the greatly reduced mail order and manufacturing operations. In 1945, in accordance with the sale agreement with L. B. Smith, The Larkin Store Corporation had regained its name of Larkin Co Inc. Under the direction of Howard H. Massing, Larkin Co Inc. continued to issue its catalogs, and many loyal customers around the nation were glad to send in their orders as in the old days. The catalog carried popular merchandise and a range of Larkin Products from perfumes to puddings, many manufactured by Larkin Products Inc. under the skillfull management of Earl Booth, son of John's trusted chemist and perfumer Clarence Booth. Nevertheless it became increasingly clear through the 1950s that the business could offer only diminishing returns. Time and change had greatly reduced the backlog of loyal secretaries, and there was no Elbert Hubbard to drum up new trade. Indeed, the world of the 1950s would have seemed strange territory to both Bert and John. In the mid-1950s, Larkin Products, Inc. was discontinued. Larkin Co Inc. continued to issue catalogs through the 1950s and the last order was shipped in January of 1962 to Mrs. Marie Miles of Philadelphia, PA. Finally, in 1967, Larkin Warehouse was sold to Graphic Controls, its largest tenant. The vision that John Larkin had when he came to Buffalo in 1875 had almost made it to the century mark. Although it could not survive, it had served the purpose John hoped for in serving his family, his employees, his customers and his city well for nearly a hundred years.

---

[1] Schlei, pp. 42,44.
[2] BECHS Larkin Company Inc. Records, *New York Women's Wear*, February 7, 1920.
[3] Schlei, pp. 36,42.
[4] 1929 sales, $15,577,564; 1930 sales $13,264,292.

[5] Conversation with Harry H. Larkin Jr., 8/3/1982.

[6] Walter F. Winters, "History of Larkin Co Inc., Larkin Warehouse Inc., Kenland Inc." 1945 pp.1–6. BECHS archives.

[7] Winters. p. 12.

[8] The instrument was dismantled and sections of it "reused in various rebuilds and installations in the Buffalo Area." BECHS, MSS Collection, David Snyder, "Historic Pipe Organs in Buffalo: a Survey."

Appendix

The following article describing the manufacture of soap appeared in *Ourselves*, June 19, 1925.

Soap in the Making

Looks Good Enough to Eat

"Toilet Requisites," a monthly magazine published in New York, has an article on the making of soap in the June issue which is so well written and so accurately describes the way Larkin Company makes soap, that we are glad to pass it on to the readers of *Ourselves*.

Volumes without number have been written upon the chemistry of soap and the slightly different processes of manufacture, but it is not necessary to go into detail concerning the chemistry of soap in order to have a thorough understanding of how some soaps are made.

"As you perhaps know, tallow, palm oil, cotton seed oil, lard oil, soya bean oil, peanut oil and olive oil are used as bases for soap manufacture. The larger percentage of soap is a combination of caustic alkali and a constituent of vegetable or animal fats called fatty acid.

"The fats, whether animal or vegetable, are ordinarily placed in large kettles, some of them holding hundreds of thousands of pounds of material. These are heated by steam coils. Caustic soda is the alkali generally used to bring about the chemical change in the fats necessary to the production of soap.

"The fats are split into two different substances by the alkali, one of which combines with alkali forming what are known as fatty acids and leaving the by product glycerin. This change in the fats takes place at the boiling point. Complete separation of the glycerin from the fatty acid is accomplished by the introduction of a saturated solution of salt. This brings about a further disassociation of glycerin and fatty acids, but this process does not remove all the impurities.

"The process of boiling in which the glycerin is freed is known as saponification. An excess of alkali hurries this chemical action and in no way hurts the soap. After being boiled the pure soap remains at the top of the kettle, the impurities and excess alkalies sinking to the bottom. These are drawn off and further treated for the extraction of glycerin. The residue, which is nearly pure soap, with a content of about 30% water, is again boiled and allowed to settle for a period of from one and one half to three days, according to the size of the kettles.

"When we speak of alkali in connection with soap manufacture, it is not meant that the finished product contains alkali, in fact pure toilet soaps contain practically no free alkali.

"Laundry soaps which are not used for bathing the face and body contain an extremely higher percentage of free alkali, as do poorly made toilet soaps.

"After the soap has been allowed to settle in the kettle, it is pumped into frames or molds holding approximately one thousand pounds of soap.

"After the soap is hardened and settled into the molds, the side and end pieces are unbolted and the soap is cut by wires into varying thicknesses, according to the brand of soap which is to be run. These slabs are further cut into blocks of the required size for stamping into wanted brands.

"Stamping, which forms the cake and impresses upon it the design or lettering, is accomplished both by hand power and mechanical means. On some grades of soap foot power presses are used, which die cut the cake ready for drying. The mechanical process differs in no great degree from the foot-power process with the exception that it produces the finished cake with more rapidity.

"Perhaps you have wondered what is meant by a 'milled soap.' This is produced by a slightly different process, the soap stock being placed in machines which are nothing more or less than a series of granite rollers which compress and refine the texture of the soap. The more milling a soap receives, the smoother it will feel to the touch and the longer it will last. The milling process expels the excess water and makes the soap less liable to shrinkage by evaporation."

The Buffalo Pottery

Of all of the subsidiary companies formed to provide premiums for Larkin Company, the most important by far was the Buffalo Pottery. Ground was broken in the spring of 1902 on property at Seneca Street and Hayes Place, and the plant went into production in the fall of 1903.

The Buffalo Pottery, originally intended to provide premiums for the Larkin catalog, soon became, under the leadership of Louis Bown and William J. Rea, one of the finest potteries in the country. It was a pioneer in the production of underglaze ware in this country, and in 1905, was the first American company to produce the popular Blue Willow pattern previously found only in English imports. In 1908, the Pottery began the production of Deldare Ware. The line, hand decorated with scenes from 18th Century English village life in rich colors against an olive-green ground, is highly prized by collectors today. In the late 1920's and 1930's, Buffalo Pottery specialized in the production of custom ware for hotels and railroads. Perhaps its finest work in that field is the 11 inch, gold-embossed service plate, with a copy of the Gilbert Stuart portrait of George Washington in its center, made for the Chesapeake and Ohio Railroad in 1932.

The Larkin family continued its interest in the Buffalo Pottery. The company name was changed to Buffalo China Inc., and Harold M. Esty Jr., a grandson of John D. Larkin, was president of the company until he retired in 1976. Buffalo China Inc. was purchased by Oneida in 1983 and continues a leader in its field. The definitive work on Buffalo Pottery is *The Book of Buffalo Pottery*, by Seymour and Violet Altman, New York: Crown Publishers, 1969.

BIBLIOGRAPHY

BOOKS

Adams, Henry. *Thomas Hart Benton, Drawing from Life*. New York: Abbeville Press, 1990.

————. *Thomas Hart Benton*. New York: Alfred A. Knop, 1989.

Art Handbook: Official Handbook of Architecture and Sculpture and Art Catalogue to the Pan-American Exposition. Buffalo, N.Y.: David Gray, 1901.

Atmore, The Rev. Charles. *The Whole Duty of Man or The Christian's Companion*. Liverpool: The Caxton Press, 1811

Banham, Reyner, et al. *Buffalo Architecture: A Guide*. Cambridge, Mass.: The MIT Press, 1981.

Benton, Thomas Hart. *An American in Art*. University of Kansas Press, 1969.

Hamilton, Charles F. *As Bees in Honey Drown: Elbert Hubbard and the Roycrofters*. New York: A. S. Barnes and Company, 1973.

"Marion Harland," *My Trip Thru The Larkin Factories*. Buffalo, N.Y.: Larkin Co., 1913.

Heath, Mary Hubbard. *The Elbert Hubbard I Knew*. East Aurora, N.Y.: The Roycrofters, 1929.

Memorial and Family History of Erie County, New York. New York-Buffalo: The Genealogical Publishing Company, 1906-8.

Larned, J. N. *A History of Buffalo*, Vol I. New York: The Progress of the Empire State Company, 1911.

Lowe, David. *The Great Chicago Fire*. New York: Dover Publications, Inc., 1979.

Martin, Darwin D. *Autobiography*. Typed Manuscript, SUNY Buffalo, Archives, Box 2, Folder 5.

————. *Diary*, SUNY Buffalo Archives.

————. *The First to Make a Card Ledger: Story of the Larkin Card Indexes*, Buffalo, N.Y., 1932.

Quinan, Jack. *Frank Lloyd Wright's Larkin Building: Myth or Fact*. New York: The Architectural History Foundation, 1987.

Ralph, Edmund S. *Chronicles of our Family*, 1894. Manuscript, copy given to me by Dorothy L. Ralph.

Souvenir of the Centennial Exhibition. Hartford, Conn.: George D. Curtis, 1877.

Winters, Walter R. *History of Larkin Co., Inc., Larkin Warehouse Inc., Kenland Inc.* 1945. BECHS Archives.

Wolfe, Milton G. *Jones Iron Works 1815–1941*. Privately published, 1981.

Wright, Frank Lloyd. *An Autobiography*. New York: Horizon Press, 1977.

JOURNALS

Ourselves. Larkin Company employee publication, BECHS collection.

The Larkin Idea. Larkin Company Journal, BECHS collection.

THESES AND DISSERTATIONS

Olson, Craig R. *The Evolution of the Larkin Company and Its Advertising Premiums, 1875–1900*. SUNY College at Oneonta, 1993.

Schlei, Mildred B. *The Larkin Company: A History*. Master's Thesis, University of Buffalo, 1932.

ARTICLES

Heath, Horton H. "Elbert Hubbard-Salesman," *Printer's Ink*. October, 1931.

Marshall, A. P. "Larkin's Departmental Farms," *The Farmer's Magazine*. Toronto, Vol. 11, No. 2, December, 1917.

Oreskovic, Johanna. "The Co-operative Ownership Plan of the Larkin Company, 1919–1921," *Studies in History*, Vol. 3. SUNY at Buffalo, 1981–1982.

Quinan, Jack. "Elbert Hubbard's Roycroft," in *Head, Heart and Hand: Elbert Hubbard and the Roycrofters*, Rochester, NY: University of Rochester Press, 1994.

Sheldon, Grace Carew. "The Balcom Homestead," *The Buffalo Evening Times*, Saturday, April 24, 1909.